VICTORIA

PO

PATTERNS & PRICES

by william heacock

Photography by

Richardson Printing Corp.

Marietta, Ohio 45750

I.S.B.N. # 0-915410-07-9

Published & Distributed by:

Antique Publications

P.O. Box 655
Marietta, Ohio 45750

Dedication

To Robert E. Richardson
who developed the idea for this book
and the staff of Richardson Printing Corporation
who put it together so beautifully.

TABLE OF CONTENTS

Title Page, Introduction, Etc. . . . . Page 1-4

Book 1 (Toothpick Holders from A to Z) . . . . Pages 5-42

Book 2 (Opalescent Glass) . . . . Pages 43-82

Book 3 (Syrups, Sugar Shakers & Cruets) . . . . . Pages 83-129

Index . . . . Pages 130-134

INTRODUCTION

This pocketbook is a miniaturized reprint of most of the color illustrations shown in the first three volumes of the "Encyclopedia of Victorian Colored Pattern Glass." Pattern names and estimated retail values are provided. However, none of the text, historical data, essays, catalogue and ad reprints, or illustrations of reproductions are provided. This information is available only in the full-size volumes.

The purposes for producing this tiny book were two-fold. It makes it possible for readers of this series to have a handy pocket edition to carry with them to antique shows, flea markets, shops and auctions. Thus, it saves wear and tear on the larger volumes. This book also makes it possible to expand the number of followers of this series, as a wealth of illustrations and pattern names are now available at a price which will appeal to any bargain hunter. The larger volumes will continue to be revised, updated and reprinted for those who wish to delve deeper into the information concerning the glass illustrated here.

Generally, there should be little confusion in using this book. An index is provided at the back which will refer you to almost any pattern which you might see advertised with a Heacock reference number. The only area where care should be taken is using these figure numbers to correspond properly with the appropriate volume number. The same basic numbers are used in volume after volume, so the book number should *always* precede the figure number to prevent confusion. Many people only own a single volume (i.e., toothpick collectors have Book 1), so please note this simple precaution.

Another word of warning. The prices provided are an estimate of general retail value. Prices always vary from area to area, from dealer to dealer. Value is determined by *how* many people with *how* much money want that item *how* badly. Add to that *how* rare the item is, and *how* much the dealer you are purchasing it from knows about all the above, and a student of market trends can determine a retail value. Some readers will feel I am too low on the prices, many will feel I am too high. It is impossible for me to avoid criticism on any level, so I have tried to provide fair market values to the best of my ability.

The prices quoted are for pieces in mint condition, and apply only to those colors illustrated. Value often varies according to the item's color. Some are rarer than others—some are more collectible.

A Rarity Guide is also provided. If only a limited number of a certain piece are known, it is labelled (S) Scarce. If two or three have been reported, it earns a respectable (R) Rare. If only one has been documented to date, it is most decidedly a (VR) Very Rare piece of glass. Rarity always adds a little value and salability to many pieces illustrated here.

An asterisk (*) by the number means the same exact item has been reproduced, not necessarily in the color shown.

4

Encyclopedia of Victorian Colored Pattern Glass

Book 1
→ Toothpick Holders from A to Z ←

by william heacock

Fig. 1
Acorn

Fig. 2
Acorn

Fig. 3
Acorn

Fig. 4
Alabama

Fig. 5
Arched Ovals

Fig. 6
Arched Ovals

Fig. 7
Argonaut
Shell

Fig. 8
Art Novo

Fig. 9
Art Novo

Fig. 10
Atlanta

Fig. 11
Atlanta

1 – $32; **2** – $65; **3** – $65; **4** – $125 (VR); **5** – $22; **6** – $28; **7** – $275 (S); **8** – $125 (R); **9** – $45; **10** – $40; **11** – $28.

Fig. 12
Banded
Portland

Fig. 13
Bellaire
Basketweave

Fig. 14
Bead & Scroll

Fig. 15
Bead & Scroll

Fig. 16
Bead Swag
or Beaded Swag

Fig. 17
Bead Swag

Fig. 18
Bead Swag

Fig. 19
Bead Swag

Fig. 20
Beaded
Grape

Fig. 21
Beaded Ovals
In Sand

Fig. 22
Beaded Panels
& Sunburst

Fig. 23
Beaded Swirl
& Disc

12 – $42; **13** – $38 (S); **14** – $35; **15** – $65 (S); **16** – $38*; **17** – $65*; **18** – $500 (VR)*;
19 – $80*; **20** – $55; **21** – $75 (S); **22** – $100 (R); **23** – $40.

Fig. 24
Beatty
Honeycomb

Fig. 25
Beatty
Ribbed Opal

Fig. 26
Bevelled Star

Fig. 27
Blocked
Thumbprint Band

Fig. 28
Bohemian

Fig. 29
Bohemian

Fig. 30
Bohemian

Fig. 31
Box-In-Box

Fig. 32
Box-In-Box

Fig. 33
Brazillian

24 – $45; **25** – $35; **26** – $60; **27** – $35; **28** – $100 (R); **29** – $85 (S); **30** – $65; **31** – $40; **32** – $40; **33** – $58.

Fig. 34
Brittanic

Fig. 35
Brilliant

Fig. 36
Bulbous Base

Fig. 37
Bulbous
Ring Neck

Fig. 38
Bulging Loops

Fig. 39
Bulging Loops

Fig. 40
Bulging Loops

Fig. 41
Bulging Loops

Fig. 42
Button Arches

Fig. 43
Button Arches

Fig. 44
Button Panel

Fig. 45
Button Panel
with Bars

34 — $50; **35** — $45; **36** — $50; **37** — $90 (R); **38** — $120 (S); **39** — $48; **40** — $150 (VR);
41 — $65; **42** — $25 (rep.); **43** — $24; **44** — $55; **45** — $95 (VR).

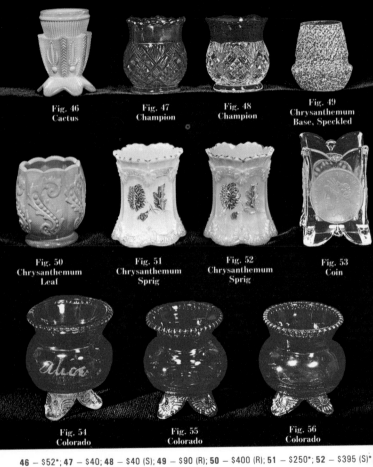

Fig. 46
Cactus

Fig. 47
Champion

Fig. 48
Champion

Fig. 49
Chrysanthemum
Base, Speckled

Fig. 50
Chrysanthemum
Leaf

Fig. 51
Chrysanthemum
Sprig

Fig. 52
Chrysanthemum
Sprig

Fig. 53
Coin

Fig. 54
Colorado

Fig. 55
Colorado

Fig. 56
Colorado

46 – $52*; **47** – $40; **48** – $40 (S); **49** – $90 (R); **50** – $400 (R); **51** – $250*; **52** – $395 (S);
53 – $100*; **54** – $24; **55** – $55; **56** – $50 (S).

10

Fig. 57
Columbian Coin

Fig. 58
Columbian Coin

Fig. 59
Columbia

Fig. 60
Cone

Fig. 61
Cone

Fig. 62
Cone

Fig. 63
Cord Drapery

Fig. 64
Cordova

Fig. 65
Cordova

Fig. 66
Cordova

57 – $175 (R); **58** – $175 (R); **59** – $50; **60** – $50; **61** – $35; **62** – $24; **63** – $500 (VR); 64 – $36; **65** – $30; **66** – $30.

Fig. 67
Cornell

Fig. 68
Creased Bale

Fig. 69
Creased Bale

Fig. 70
Croesus

Fig. 71
Cut Block

Daisy & Button
(See Figs. 78-92)

Fig. 72
Delaware

Fig. 73
Delaware

Fig. 74
Diamond
Spearhead

Fig. 75
Diamond
Spearhead

Fig. 76
Diamond
Spearhead

Fig. 77
Diamond
Spearhead

67 – $45; **68** – $35; **69** – $55; **70** – $90*; **71** – $45; **72** – $80; **73** – $110 (S); **74** – $7⸱
75 – $48; **76** – $55; **77** – $100 (R).

12

DAISY & BUTTON

Fig. 78
Daisy
& Button
(Hobbs)

Fig. 79
Daisy
& Button
(Hobbs)

Fig. 80
Daisy
& Button
(Plain)

Fig. 81
D & B
Figural

Fig. 82
D & B
Figural

Fig. 83 D & B
Figural

Fig. 84
D & B
Figural

Fig. 85
D & B
Figural

Fig. 86
D & B
Figural

Fig. 87
D & B
Figural

Fig. 88
D & B
Figural

Fig. 89
Daisy
& Button
(Duncan)

Fig. 90
Daisy
& Button
with Red Dots

Fig. 91
Daisy & Button
With
V-Ornament

Fig. 92
Daisy & Button
With
V-Ornament

78 – $35*; **79** – $28*; **80** – $28; **81** – $35*; **82** – $28; **83** – $26; **84** – $32; **85** – $28; **86** – $48; **87** – $40; **88** – $55; **89** – $35; **90** – $55; **91** – $38; **92** – $38.

Fig. 93
Diamond
with Peg.

Fig. 94
Diamond
with Peg.

Fig. 95
Double Arch

Fig. 96
Double Circle

Fig. 97
Double Circle

Fig. 98
Double Dahlia
with Lens

Fig. 99
Double Dahlia
with Lens

Fig. 100
Doyle's
Honeycomb

Fig. 101
Draped Beads

Fig. 102
Ellipses

93 — $26; **94** — $50; **95** — $60 (S); **96** — $45; **97** — $55 (S); **98** — $40; **99** — $90 (S); **100** — $40 (S); **101** — $22; **102** — $55.

Fig. 103
Empress

Fig. 104
Esther

Fig. 105
Esther

Fig. 106
Eureka
National's

Fig. 107
Famous

Fig. 108
Fancy Loop

Fig. 109
Feather

Fig. 110
Feather

Fig. 111
Flora

03 – $125 (S); **104** – $75; **105** – $75; **106** – $65 (S); **107** – $65 (VR); **108** – $75; **109** – $150 (VR); **110** – $100 (R); **111** – $100 (R).

Fig. 112
Florette

Fig. 113
Florette

Fig. 114
Florette

Fig. 115
Florette

Fig. 116
Florida

Fig. 117
Flower
& Pleat

Fig. 118
Flower
& Pleat

Fig. 119
Flute, Northwood's

Fig. 120
Flute, Northwood's

Fig. 121
Flute, Northwood's

112 — $55 (S); **113** — $85 (R); **114** — $75 (R); **115** — $28; **116** — $145 (VR); **117** — $38; **118** — $90 (R); **119** — $70 (R); **120** — $50*; **121** — $85*.

Fig. 122
Forget-Me-Not

Fig. 123
Forget-Me-Not

Fig. 124
Frances
Ware Swirl

Fig. 125
Frazier

Fig. 126
Geneva

Fig. 127
Geneva

Fig. 128
Geneva

Fig. 129
Georgia Gem

Fig. 130
Georgia Gem

22 — $45; 123 — $35; 124 — $85 (S); 125 — $50; 126 — $90 (R); 127 — $400 (VR); 128 — $80 S); 129 — $60; 130 — $50 (S).

Fig. 131
Gold Band

Fig. 132
Gonterman
Swirl

Fig. 133
Gonterman
Swirl

Fig. 134
Gonterman
Swirl

Fig. 135
Guttate

Fig. 136
Guttate

Fig. 137
Guttate

Souvenir of
Fennville, Mich.

Ethel

Fig. 138
Harvard

Fig. 139
Harvard

Fig. 140
Harvard

131 – $50; **132** – $80 (S); **133** – $175 (VR); **134** – $135 (R); **135** – $88 (R); **136** – $38
137 – $50; **138** – $35; **139** – $35; **140** – $32.

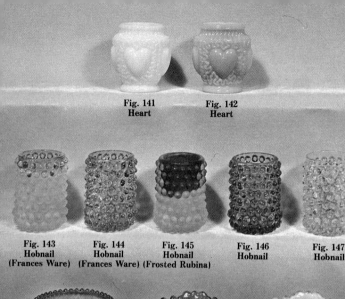

Fig. 141
Heart

Fig. 142
Heart

Fig. 143
Hobnail
(Frances Ware)

Fig. 144
Hobnail
(Frances Ware)

Fig. 145
Hobnail
(Frosted Rubina)

Fig. 146
Hobnail

Fig. 147
Hobnail

Fig. 148
Holly Amber

Fig. 149
Idyll

Fig. 150
Idyll

141 − $22; **142** − $55; **143** − $48; **144** − $42; **145** − $175 (VR); **146** − $28; **147** − $25;
148 − $300 (S)*; **149** − $70; **150** − $175 (R).

Fig. 151
Inverted Fan
& Feather

Fig. 152
Inverted
Thumbprint

Fig. 153
Inverted
Thumbprint

Fig. 154
Iris
with Meander

Fig. 155
Iris
with Meander

Fig. 156
Iris
with Meander

Fig. 157
Iris
with Meander

Fig. 158
Iris
with Meander

151 — $575 (R)*; **152** — $35; **153** — $50; **154** — $48; **155** — $45; **156** — $85 (S); **157** — $60
158 — $36.

Fig. 159
Ivy, Sandwich

Fig. 160
Jewelled Heart

Fig. 161
Kentucky

Fig. 162
Kittens

Fig. 163
Klondike

Fig. 164
Lacy Medallion

Fig. 165
Lacy Medallion

Fig. 166
Lacy Medallion

Fig. 167
Leaf and Star

Fig. 168
Leaf Bracket

159 — $95 (R); **160** — $50 (S) (rep.); **161** — $55; **162** — $90; **163** — $350 (S); **164** — $24*;
165 — $26*; **166** — $26*; **167** — $35 (S); **168** — $90.

Fig. 169
Leaf Mold

Fig. 170
Leaf Mold

Fig. 171
Leaf Mold

Fig. 172
Leaf Mold

Fig. 173
Leaf Mold

Fig. 174
Leaf Mold

Fig. 175
Leaf Mold

Fig. 176
Leaf Umbrella

Fig. 177
Leaf Umbrella

Fig. 178
Leaf Umbrella

Fig. 179
Leaf Umbrella

169 – $110; **170** – $80; **171** – $120 (S); **172** – $140 (R); **173** – $95 (S); **174** – $135 (VR); **175** – $65 (S); **176** – $80 (S); **177** – $125 (S); **178** – $85; **179** – $120 (S).

Fig. 180
Maple Leaf

Fig. 181
Maize

Fig. 182
Majestic

Fig. 183
Medallion Sprig

Fig. 184
Medallion Sprig

Fig. 185
Nestor

Fig. 186
New Hampshire

Fig. 187
One-O-One

180 — $650 (R)*; **181** — $275 (R); **182** — $65; **183** — $120 (R); **184** — $110 (R); **185** — $65 (S); **186** — $38; **187** — $55.

OPALESCENT BLOWN PATTERNS

Fig. 188
Bubble

Fig. 189
Chrysanthemum
Base Swirl

Fig. 190
Chrysanthemum
Base Swirl

Fig. 191
Criss-Cross

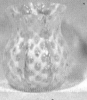

Fig. 192
Criss-Cross

Fig. 193
Criss-Cross

Fig. 194
Daisy and Fern

Fig. 195
Daisy and Fern

Fig. 196
Fern, Ribbed

188 — $78; **189** — $110 (S); **190** — $85 (S); **191** — $125 (R); **192** — $40; **193** — $110 (S); **194** — $95 (S); **195** — $135 (R); **196** — $48 (S).

OPALESCENT BLOWN PATTERNS

Fig. 197
Labelle Opal

Fig. 198
Lattice,
Ribbed Opalescent

Fig. 199
Lattice,
Ribbed Opalescent

Fig. 200
Lattice,
Ribbed Opalescent

Fig. 201
Polka Dot

Fig. 202
Seaweed

Fig. 203
Sprig,
Panelled Opalescent

Fig. 204
Stripe

197 — $75; 198 — $65; 199 — $85 (S); 200 — $30; 201 — $200 (VR); 202 — $185 (VR); 203 — $38; 204 — $28.

OPALESCENT BLOWN PATTERNS

Fig. 205	Fig. 206	Fig. 207	Fig. 208
Swirl,	Swirl,	Swirl,	Swirl,
Opalescent Reverse	Opalescent Reverse	Opalescent Reverse	Opalescent Reverse

Fig. 209
Swirl,
Opalescent

Fig. 210
Swirl,
Opalescent

Fig. 211
Windows,
Opalescent

Fig. 212
Windows,
Opalescent

Fig. 213
Wide Stripe,
Opalescent

205 — $75 (S); **206** — $58; **207** — $70 (S); **208** — $110 (R); **209** — $55 (S); **210** — $75 (S); **211** — $95; **212** — $80; **213** — $58 (S).

Fig. 214
Optic

Fig. 215
Optic, Pressed

Fig. 216
Optic,
West Virginia's

Fig. 217
Orinda

Fig. 218
Orinda

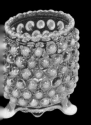

Fig. 219
Over-All
Hobnail

Fig. 220
Over-All
Hobnail

Fig. 221
Over-All
Hobnail

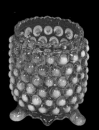

Fig. 222
Over-All
Hobnail

214 — $45; 215 — $55 (S); 216 — $35; 217 — $85 (S); 218 — $30 (S); 219 — $28 (White); 220 — $55 (S); 221 — $35; 222 — $42.

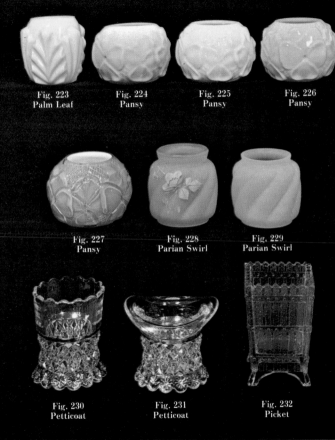

Fig. 223
Palm Leaf

Fig. 224
Pansy

Fig. 225
Pansy

Fig. 226
Pansy

Fig. 227
Pansy

Fig. 228
Parian Swirl

Fig. 229
Parian Swirl

Fig. 230
Petticoat

Fig. 231
Petticoat

Fig. 232
Picket

223 – $32; **224** – $55 (S); **225** – $38; **226** – $35; **227** – $65 (R); **228** – $32; **229** – $45
230 – $65 (S); **231** – $70 (R); **232** – $60 (S).

Fig. 233
Pillar

Fig. 234
Pillar

Fig. 235
Pineapple
& Fan

Fig. 236
Pineapple
& Fan

Fig. 237
Plain Scalloped
Panel

Fig. 238
Plain Scalloped
Panel

Fig. 239
Plain Scalloped
Panel

Fig. 240
Pleating

Fig. 241
Prince Albert

Fig. 242
Prince of
Wales Plumes

233 – $95 (S); 234 – $48; 235 – $120 (S); 236 – $110 (R); 237 – $24; 238 – $35 (S); 239 – $45; 240 – $32; 241 – $75 (VR); 242 – $195 (S).

Fig. 243
Prize, The

Fig. 244
Prize, The

Fig. 245
Punty Band

Fig. 246
Quilted
Phlox

Fig. 247
Quilted
Phlox

Fig. 248
Reverse Swirl,
Speckled

Fig. 249
Rib & Bead

Fig. 250
Ribbed Drape

Fig. 251
Ribbed Drape

Fig. 252
Ribbed Spiral

Fig. 253
Ribbed Spiral

Fig. 254
Ribbed
Thumbprint

243 — $55 (S); **244** — $55 (S); **245** — $45; **246** — $55 (S); **247** — $52 (S); **248** — $35; **249** — $45
250 — $145 (S); **251** — $100 (R); **252** — $65; **253** — $75; **254** — $24.

Fig. 255
Ring Band

Fig. 256
Ring Band

Fig. 257
Ring Base

Fig. 258
Ring Base

Fig. 259
Royal, Co-op's

Fig. 260
Royal, Co-op's

Fig. 261
Royal, King's

Fig. 262
Royal Ivy

Fig. 263
Royal Ivy

Fig. 264
Royal Ivy

Fig. 265
Royal Ivy

Fig. 266
Royal Ivy

255 – $110 (S); **256** – $85; **257** – $48; **258** – $75; **259** – $28; **260** – $24; **261** – $20; **262** – $85; **263** – $120; **264** – $135 (R); **265** – $95 (S); **266** – $125 (R).

Fig. 267
Royal Oak

Fig. 268
Royal Oak

Fig. 269
Ruby
Thumbprint

Fig. 270
Ruby
Thumbprint

Fig. 271
Saxon

Fig. 272
Scalloped
Six-Point

Fig. 273
Scalloped
Skirt

Fig. 274
Scalloped
Skirt

Fig. 275
Scalloped
Swirl

Fig. 276
Scalloped
Swirl

267 – $135 (S); **268** – $90 (S); **269** – $58 (R); **270** – $40; **271** – $32; **272** – $50 (S); **273** – $38; **274** – $45; **275** – $38; **276** – $38.

Fig. 277
Scroll
with Acanthus

Fig. 278
Scroll
with Acanthus

Fig. 279
Scroll
with Acanthus

Fig. 280
Scroll with
Cane Band

Fig. 281
Scroll with
Cane Band

Fig. 282
Scroll with
Cane Band

Fig. 283
Serrated Ribs
& Panels

Fig. 284
Shamrock
Souvenir

Fig. 285
Shamrock
Souvenir

Fig. 286
Shell

Fig. 287
Shoeshone

277 – $95 (R); **278** – $85 (S); **279** – $65 (S); **280** – $55; **281** – $48; **282** – $45; **283** – $45); **284** – $24; **285** – $28; **286** – $300 (VR); **287** – $55.

Fig. 288
Spearpoint
Band

Fig. 289
Sprig,
Panelled

Fig. 290
S Repeat

Fig. 291
S Repeat

Fig. 292
Summit, The

Fig. 293
Sunbeam

Fig. 294
Sunbeam

Fig. 295
Sunset

Fig. 296
Sunk Honeycomb

288 — $38; **289** — $95 (R); **290** — repro?; **291** — $38*; **292** — $52 (S); **293** — $60 (R); **294** — $3
295 — $38; **296** — $38.

Fig. 297
Swag
with Brackets

Fig. 298
Swag
with Brackets

Fig. 299
Swag
with Brackets

Fig. 300
Swag
with Brackets

Fig. 301
Swirl,
Princess

Fig. 302
Swirl,
Two-Ply

Fig. 303
Swirl and Leaf

Fig. 304
Thompson's
No. 77

Fig. 305
Thousand Eye

Fig. 306
Thumbprint,
Tarentum's

Fig. 307
Tiny Optic

Fig. 308
Tiny Optic

297 – $135 (R)*; **298** – $95 (S)*; **299** – $75*; **300** – $48*; **301** – $38; **302** – $35; **303** – $40;
304 – $35; **305** – $38; **306** – $85 (S); **307** – $35*; **308** – $34*.

Fig. 309
Tokyo

Fig. 310
Tokyo

Fig. 311
Twist

Fig. 312
U.S. Rib

Fig. 313
Virginia or
Galloway

Fig. 314
Venetian
Diamond

Fig. 315
Vermont

Fig. 316
Vermont

Fig. 317
Washington

Fig. 318
Washington

Fig. 319
Washington

309 – $100 (S); **310** – $80; **311** – $70 (S); **312** – $38; **313** – $58 (S)*; **314** – $195 (S); **315** – $85*; **316** – $50*; **317** – $30; **318** – $28; **319** – $85 (S).

Fig. 320
Wedding Bells

Fig. 321
Wild Bouquet

Fig. 322
Wild Bouquet

Fig. 323
Wild Rose
with Scrolling

Fig. 324
Wild Rose
with Scrolling

Fig. 325
Winged Scroll

Fig. 326
Winged Scroll

Fig. 327
Winged Scroll

Fig. 328
Winged Scroll

320 – $75 (R); **321** – $175 (S); **322** – $650 (VR); **323** – $135 (R); **324** – $75 (R); **325** – $95;
326 – $195 (R); **327** – $145 (R); **328** – $100 (S).

Fig. 329
Wreath & Shell

Fig. 330
Wreath & Shell

Fig. 331
Wreath & Shell

Fig. 332
X-Ray

Fig. 333
X-Ray

Fig. 334
Zanesville

Fig. 335
Zipper
Slash

Fig. 336
Zipper
Slash

329 – $125; **330** – $80; **331** – $145; **332** – $75 (S); **333** – $45; **334** – $32; **335** – $28
336 – $60.

ADDENDA 1
SCARCE IN COLOR

Fig. 337
Carnation,
New Martinsville's

Fig. 338
Hickman

Fig. 339
Iowa

Fig. 340
Massachusetts

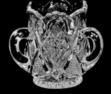

Fig. 341
Minnesota

Fig. 342
Pennsylvania

Fig. 343
Stars
and Bars

Fig. 345
Tacoma

In Color or Color-stained only: **337** — $150 (VR); **338** — $75 (S); **339** — $50 (S); **340** — $125 (R);
341 — $100 (R); **342** — $85 (R); **343** — $85 (S); **345** — $68 (R).

Fig. 346
Button Arches

Fig. 347
Croesus

Fig. 348
D & M #42

Fig. 349
Delaware

Fig. 350
Double Greek Key

Fig. 351
Georgia Gem

Fig. 352
Iowa

Fig. 353
Nestor

Fig. 354
Pillar,
Ribbed

346 – $35; **347** – $75*; **348** – $85 (R); **349** – $75; **350** – $95 (R); **351** – $75 (S); **352** – $50 (S); **353** – $65 (R); **354** – $45.

Fig. 355
Plain Band

Fig. 356
Ribbed Thumbprint

Fig. 357
S Repeat

Fig. 358
Shell &
Seaweed

Fig. 359
Texas

Fig. 360
Threaded
Rubina

Fig. 361
Vermont

Fig. 362
Virginia or Galloway

355 — $28; **356** — $48; **357** — $58*; **358** — $55; **359** — $80 (R); **360** — $85 (R); **361** — $90 (R); **362** — $38*.

(MISCELLANEOUS TOOTHPICKS OF INTEREST)

Fig. 363
Victorian
Lady

Fig. 364
Three-Dolphin
Match

Fig. 365
Brownie
Under Umbrella

Fig. 366
Rat By
A Pouch

Fig. 367
Mary Gregory

Fig. 368
Sunbonnet
Babies

Fig. 369
Owl on
Branch

Fig. 370
Wavecrest

Fig. 371
Polka Dot
Rose

Fig. 372
Snake on
a Stump

Fig. 373
BPOE Novelty

363 – $75; **364** – $65; **365** – $195 (VR); **366** – $85 (S); **367** – $48; **368** – $300 (R); **369** – $80;
370 – $175; **371** – $195 (VR); **372** – $75; **373** – $85 (R).

Encyclopedia of
Victorian Colored Pattern Glass

Book II
OPALESCENT GLASS from A to Z

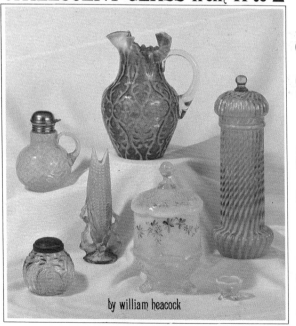

by william heacock

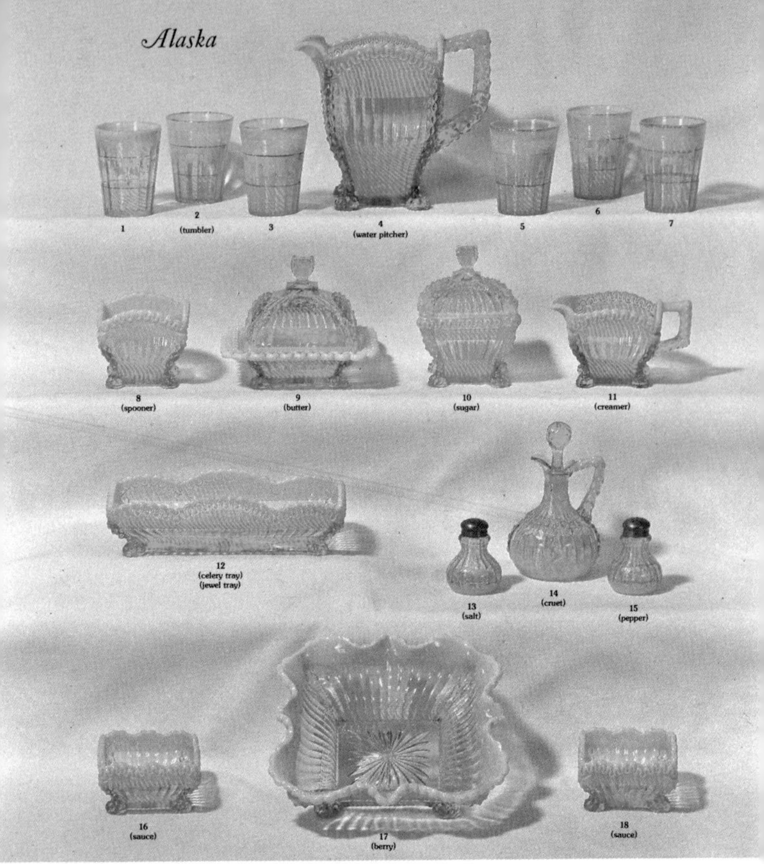

Alaska

1
2
(tumbler)
3
4
(water pitcher)
5
6
7

8
(spooner)
9
(butter)
10
(sugar)
11
(creamer)

12
(celery tray)
(jewel tray)
13
(salt)
14
(cruet)
15
(pepper)

16
(sauce)
17
(berry)
18
(sauce)

1 — $55; **4** — $350 (S); **8** — $55; **9** — $225; **10** — $150; **11** — $55; **12** — $150 (S); **13** — $45-50 ea.; **14** — $250-300 (S); **16** — $25; **17** — $85.

Everglades

19
(spooner)

20
(butter)

21
(creamer)

22
(sugar)

23
(water pitcher)

24
(tumbler)

Jewel & Flower

25
(water pitcher)

26
(spooner)

27
(butter)

28
(sugar)

29
(creamer)

Wild Bouquet

30
(sauce)

31
(berry)

32
(jelly)

33
(tumbler)

34
(water pitcher)

35
(spooner)

36
(butter)

37
(sugar)

38
(creamer)

19 — $85; **20** — $250-300 (S); **21** — $75; **22** — $165; **23** — $375-400 (R); **24** — $75; **25** — $450-550 (R); **26** — $95; **27** — $250-300; **28** — $195; **29** — $75; **30** — $30; **31** — $100; **32** — $95 (R); **33** — $95 (S); **34** — $285; **35** — $90; **36** — $300 (VR); **37** — $200 (R); **38** — $80.

Inverted Jan & Jeather

| 39 (creamer) | 40 (butter) | 41 (sugar) | 42 (spooner) | 43 (water pitcher) | 44 (tumbler) |

Intaglio

| 45 (creamer) | 46 (butter) | 47 (spooner) | 48 (water pitcher) | 49 (tumbler) |

Intaglio

| 50 (water tray) | 51 (sauce) | 52 (berry) | (sauce) |

Beatty Swirl

39 — $120 (S); **40** — $375 (VR); **41** — $225 (VR)*; **42** — $125 (S); **43** — $500 (VR); **44** — $100 (S); **45** — $55; **46** — $350 (R); **47** — $75; **48** — $250 (S); **49** — $75 (R); **50** — $95 (S); **51** — $30; **52** — $195 (R).

Circled Scroll

53
(sauce)

54
(berry)

(sauce)

55
(water pitcher)

56
(tumbler)

57
(salt)

58
(jelly)

(pepper)

59
(spooner)

60
(butter)

61
(creamer)

62
(sugar)

Beatty Swirl

Scroll with Acanthus

63
(water pitcher)

64
(sugar)

65
(water pitcher)

66
(jelly)

S-Repeat

Panelled Holly

67
(berry)

68
(spooner)

69
(creamer)

53 — $35; **54** — $85 (S); **55** — $265 (S); **56** — $75; **57** — $65 (R); **58** — $85 (VR); **59** — $75 (S);
60 — $275 (VR); **61** — $75; **62** — $150 (S); **63** — $145 (S); **64** — $80; **65** — $275 (S); **66** — $35;
67 — $85; **68** — $95 (S); **69** — $95 (S).

Wreath & Shell
& Other
Albany Glass

70
(celery)

71
(cracker jar)

72
(tumbler, footed)

73
(water pitcher)

74
(tumbler, collared)

75
(creamer)

76
(sugar)

77
(butter)

78
(spooner)

79
(toothpick)

Ribbed Spiral

80
(jelly)

81
(cup & saucer)

82
(covered sugar)

83
(lady's spittoon)

84
(rose bowl)

85
(sauce)

86
(berry)

(sauce)

87
(bon-bon)

70 – $110; **71** – $400 (VR); **72** – $65 (VR); **73** – $350 (R); **74** – $60 (S); **75** – $85 (R); **76** – $125; **77** – $185; **78** – $65; **79** – $135 (S); **80** – $48; **81** – $75 (R); **82** – $125 (VR); **83** – $48; **84** – $55; **85** – $24; **86** – $85; **87** – $40.

Swag with Brackets

88 (tumbler) 89 (pitcher) (tumbler)

Panelled Holly
(water pitcher)

Swag with Brackets

91 (creamer) 92 (sugar) 93 (butter) 94 (spooner)

Frosted Leaf & Basketweave

95 (spooner) 96 (butter) 97 (sugar) 98 (creamer)

*Hobnail &
Panelled Thumbprint*
(sauce)
99

Everglades
(master berry)
100

Daisy & Greek Key
(sauce)
101

88 – $65 (R); 89 – $220 (S); 90 – $450 (VR); 91 – $55; 92 – $110; 93 – $165; 94 – $65;
95 – $85 (R); 96 – $195 (R); 97 – $125 (R); 98 – $85 (R); 99 – $20; 100 – $150; 101 – $22.

102 (water pitcher)

103 (tumbler)

Fluted Scrolls
& *"Jackson"*

Jackson (water pitcher)

104

105 (powder or puff jar)

106 (butter)

107 (spooner)

108 (sugar)

109 (creamer)

110 (salt)

111 (spooner)

112 (butter)

113 (sugar)

114 (creamer)

115 (water pitcher)

Drapery

116 (sauce)

117 (berry)

(sauce)

118 (tumbler)

102 – $200; **103** – $55; **104** – $225; **105** – $50; **106** – $185; **107** – $55 (S); **108** – $110; **109** – $45; **110** – $45; **111** – $65; **112** – $195; **113** – $125; **114** – $65; **115** – $195; **116** – $28; **117** – $85; **118** – $40.

Palm Beach

119
(sugar)

120
(creamer)

121
(butter)

122
(spooner)

123
(tumbler)

124
(pitcher)

125
(sauce)

126
(finger bowl)

127
(butter)

Jan

128
(sugar)

129
(celery)
Beatty Rib

130
(syrup)
Diamond Spearhead

131 (spooner)
N. Regal

132
(tumbler)
S - Repeat

133
(jelly)
Tokyo

134
(jelly)
Intaglio

135
(jelly)
Swag / Brackets

136
(cruet; n.o.s.)
Argonaut Shell

19 – $165 (S); **120** – $95; **121** – $275 (R); **122** – $75; **123** – $75 (S); **124** – $300 (R); **25** – $28; **126** – $35; **127** – $250 (VR); **128** – $150 (VR); **129** – $75; **130** – $225 (R); **31** – $55; **132** – $40 (R); **133** – $30; **134** – $35; **135** – $28; **136** – $235 (S).

An Assortment . . .

137
Honeycomb
with Clover

138
Dolly Madison

139
Iris with Meander

140
Double Greek Key

141
Flute

142
Frosted Leaf &
Basketweave

143
Northwood's Regal

144
Argonaut Shell

145
Shell

146
Jewelled Heart

147
Waterlily with
Cattails

148
Northwood's
Regal

149
Idyll

150
Tokyo

151
Waterlily with
Cattails
(tumbler)

152
Jewelled
Heart
(sauce)

153
Acorn Burrs
(sauce)

154
Argonaut Shell
(sauce)

155
Iris with
Meander
(tumbler)

137 – $225 (VR); **138** – $250 (VR); **139** – $210 (S); **140** – $250 (S); **141** – repro; **142** – $225 (R); **143** – $225 (S); **144** – $275 (VR)*; **145** – $200 (VR); **146** – $125 (R)*; **147** – $110 (VR); **148** – $100; **149** – $125 (S); **150** – $90; **151** – $50; **152** – $28; **153** – $35 (VR); **154** – $38*; **155** – $45.

Hobnail & Thousand Eye

156
Hobnail, 4 Ft.
(sugar)
(non-opalescent)

157
*Hobnail_
in_Square*
(barber bottle)

158
Hobnail
(Hobbs)

159
Hobnail
(Hobbs)
(butter)

160
Over_All Hob
(pitcher)

Thousand Eye

161
(creamer)

162
(spooner)

163
(celery vase)

164
(water pitcher)

165
Over_All Hob
(creamer)

166
*Gonterman
Hob*
(cruet, n.o.s.)

167
Northwood's Hobnail
(spooner)

168
Hobnail
(water pitcher)

169
*Over_All
Hob*
(tumbler)

156 – $60; **157** – $60 (VR); **158** – $120; **159** – $110*; **160** – $150 (S); **161** – $50; **162** – $65; **163** – $85; **164** – $125; **165** – $45; **166** – $200 (R); **167** – $25; **168** – $65; **169** – $35.

Curtain Call
(castor set)

Ribbed Spiral
(water set)

Gonterman Swirl

173
(syrup)

174
(spooner)

175
(sugar)

176
(pitcher)

177
(tumbler)

178

Gonterman Swirl
(gas shade)

179

*Diamond
Spearhead*
(indiv. creamer)

180

*Finecut &
Roses*
(spooner)

181

*Buttons &
Braids*
(pressed tumbler)

182

*Christmas
Pearls*
(cruet)

183

Sunburst – on – Shield
(covered sugar)

184

Sunburst – on – Shield
(breakfast sugar)

185

(breakfast creamer)

186

Beauty Swirl
(butter)

170 – $275 (VR); **171** – $55 (S); **172** – $275 (VR); **173** – $235 (VR); **174** – $80 (S); **175** – $135; **176** – $265 (VR); **177** – $55 (S); **178** – $58; **179** – $55; **180** – $28; **181** – $28; **182** – $175 (VR); **183** – $150 (R); **184** – $48; **185** – $48; **186** – $125 (R).

An Assortment . . .

187
Stripe
(castor set, 5 bottles)

188
Waterlily with Cattails
(pitcher)

189
Stripe
(castor set)

190
Sunburst-on-Shield
(butter)

191
Wild Bouquet
(cruet)

192
Diamond Spearhead
(goblet)

193
Shell
(butter)

194
Beatty Honeycomb
(celery vase)

195
Gonterman Swirl
(celery vase)

196
Northwood Block
(celery vase)

197
Scroll with Acanthus
(rare green)

198
Jewelled Heart
(tumbler)

199
Idyll
(spooner)

200
Duchess
(gas shade)

201
Scroll with Acanthus
(canary)

187 — $175 (S); **188** — $250; **189** — $120 (S); **190** — $250 (VR); **191** — $275 (R); **192** — $65 (R); **193** — $400 (VR); **194** — $65 (S); **195** — $135; **196** — $38; **197** — $38 (S); **198** — $24; **199** — $95; **200** — $65; **201** — $55.

203
N. Town Pump

204
N. Trough

205
Ribbed Spiral
(spooner)

202
Alaska
(banana boat)

208
Shell
(creamer)

209
Flora
(butter)

206
(butter)
Double Greek Key

207
(toothpick)

211
N. Maple Leaf
(jelly)

212
Diamond Spearhead
(spooner)

210
Old Man Winter
(small basket)

213
Beatty Ribbed Opal

214
N. Peacocks on a Fence
(salad)

202 – $265 (R); **203** – $85*; **204** – $50*; **205** – $60; **206** – $185 (R); **207** – $95 (R); **208** – $100 (S); **209** – $100; **210** – $50; **211** – $52; **212** – $55; **213** – $125 (S); **214** – $85.

Cruets, Etc. . . . .

(PRESSED & BLOWN)

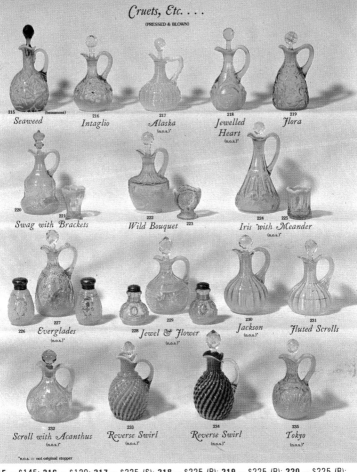

215 (beaumont)
Seaweed

216
Intaglio

217
Alaska
(n.o.s.)*

218
*Jewelled
Heart*
(n.o.s.)*

219
Flora

220
221
Swag with Brackets

222
223
Wild Bouquet

224
225
Iris with Meander
(n.o.s.)*

226
227
Everglades
(n.o.s.)*

228
229
Jewel & Flower
(n.o.s.)*

230
Jackson
(n.o.s.)*

231
Fluted Scrolls

232
Scroll with Acanthus
(n.o.s.)*

233
Reverse Swirl
(n.o.s.)*

234
Reverse Swirl
(n.o.s.)*

235
Tokyo
(n.o.s.)*

*n.o.s. = not original stopper

215 – $145; **216** – $130; **217** – $225 (S); **218** – $225 (R); **219** – $225 (R); **220** – $225 (R); **221** – $135 (S); **222** – $235 (R); **223** – $175 (S); **224** – $215 (R); **225** – $75; **226** – $75 (R); **227** – $250 (S); **228** – $75 (S); **229** – $225; **230** – $120; **231** – $120; **232** – $150; **233** – $120; **234** – $175; **235** – $150.

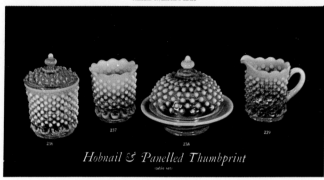

Hobnail & Panelled Thumbprint

(table set)

240
(butter)

241
(creamer)

Lustre Flute

236 — $85; **237** — $60; **238** — $125; **239** — $55; **240** — $85; **241** — $45.

Ribbed Opal Lattice

Reverse Swirl

246
(sugar
shaker)

244
(tumbler)

245
(mustard)

247
(toothpick)

248
(salt
shaker)

242
(tumbler)

243
(pitcher)

Chrysanthemum Base Swirl

(unfrosted)

249
(salt)

(pepper)

250
(toothpick)

251
(cruet)

252
(covered butter)

253
(covered sugar)

254
(celery base)

Opalescent Seaweed

255
(sugar)

257
(creamer)

258 (celery vase)

259
(pitcher)

256
(spooner)

260
(toothpick)

262
(oil cruet)

264
(tumbler)

261
(salt
shaker)

263
(sugar shaker)

242 – $55; **243** – $245 (S); **244** – $50; **245** – $55; **246** – $110; **247** – $110; **248** – $32; **249** – $32; **250** – $110; **251** – $195; **252** – $235 (S); **253** – $165 (S); **254** – $110; **255** – $125; **256** – $75; **257** – $80; **258** – $95; **259** – $275 (R); **260** – $185 (VR); **261** – $45; **262** – $200; **263** – $145; **264** – $48.

Pitchers & Tumblers . . .

265
Twist
(blown)

266
Arabian Nights

267
Coinspot

268
Coinspot
(square-top)

269
Stripe
(ring-neck)

270
Criss-Cross
(Consolidated's)

271
Daisy & Fern
(Northwood)

272

273
Poinsettia
(water set)
(squatty shape)

265 — $175 (S); **266** — $235 (R); **267** — $110; **268** — $120; **269** — $160 (R); **270** — $300 (R); **271** — $185 (S); **272** — $28; **273** — $145.

Pitchers & Tumblers . . .

274
Swirling Maize

275
Honeycomb

276   *Spanish Lace*   277

278
Poinsettia
(tankard shape)

279

280
Buttons & Braids

281   *Buttons & Braids*
282

274 – $195 (VR); **275** – $185; **276** – $58; **277** – $265 (S); **278** – $145; **279** – $30; **280** – $130; **281** – $50; **282** – $245.

Opalescent Stripe
(unique opal. handle)

Reverse Swirl

Daisy & Fern

N. Daisy & Fern
(pitcher)
(tumbler)

Seaweed

Windows, Plain

Bullseye
(water carafe)

Reverse Swirl
(creamer)

Onyx Findlay
(vase) (spooner)

Opal. Swirl
(rubina)

Opal. Herringbone

Fern, Ribbed
(toothpick)

Daisy & Fern
(Apple Blossom mold)
(spooner)

(toothpick)
53

Bubble Lattice
(or "Windows")
(finger bowl)

283 – $175 (R); **284** – $160; **285** – $135; **286** – $245 (S); **287** – $50; **288A** – $120;
288B – $125; **289** – $235 (S); **290** – $125 (S); **291** – $85; **292** – $400 (VR); **293** – $500 (VR);
294 – $30*; **295** – $55; **296** – $150 (R); **297** – $75; **298** – $100 (R); **299** – $45*.

Opal. Fern
(pitcher)

Opal. Swirl
(pitcher)

Daisy & Fern
(pitcher)

Opal. Swirl
(tankard)
(Beaumont)

Opal. Swirl
(rose bowl)
(Jefferson)

Coinspot & Swirl
(syrup)

Daisy & Fern
(optic mold)

Reverse Swirl
(lamp)

Baby Coinspot
(syrup)

Spanish Lace
(butter)

Opal. Swastika
(water set)

300 — $155; **301** — $110; **302** — $135; **303** — $145; **304** — $120, **305** — $40*; **306** — $120;
307 — $105; **308** — $195; **309** — $28 (R); **310** — $150 (VR); **311** — $85 (S).

312
(pitcher)

313
(cruet)

Opal. Herringbone

Reverse Swirl
(butter)
314

315
Christmas Snowflake
(pitcher)

316
Windows
(spooner)

317
(t.p.)

318
(syrup)

Consolidated Criss-Cross

319
(t.p.)

320
(syrup)

321
(tumbler)

Daisy in Criss-Cross

325
Opal. Swirl
(cruet)

322
(salt & pepper)

Spanish Lace

323 (finger bowl)

324
(sugar shaker)

312 — $300 (R); **313** — $175 (S); **314** — $120 (S); **315** — $350 (R); **316** — $85; **317** — $150 (S);
318 — $395 (VR); **319** — $165; **320** — $300 (S); **321** — $48; **322** — $50 ea.; **323** — $40;
324 — $90; **325** — $100.

Hobnail by Hobbs, Brockunier & Co.

326
(lemonade pitcher)

327
(water pitcher)
(old reeded handle)

332
(creamer)

333
(bride's basket)

328
syrup
(rubina)

329
(milk pitcher)

330
(celery)

331
(tumbler)

334
syrup
(cranberry)

335
(cruet)

336
(barber bottle)

340
lemonade set
(on original tray)

337
(berry bowl)

338
(berry sauce)

339
(miniature
water pitcher)

326 – $220; **327** – $200; **328** – $175; **329** – $165 (R); **330** – $95; **331** – $55; **332** – $55; **333** – $400 (R); **334** – $210; **335** – $200; **336** – $90; **337** – $95*; **338** – $35*; **339** – $165 (R); **340** – $475 set.

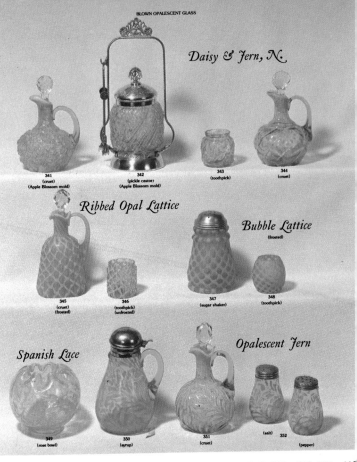

BLOWN OPALESCENT GLASS

Daisy & Fern, N.

341
(cruet)
(Apple Blossom mold)

342
(pickle castor)
(Apple Blossom mold)

343
(toothpick)

344
(cruet)

Ribbed Opal Lattice

Bubble Lattice
(frosted)

345
(cruet)
(frosted)

346
(toothpick)
(unfrosted)

347
(sugar shaker)

348
(toothpick)

Spanish Lace

Opalescent Fern

349
(rose bowl)

350
(syrup)

351
(cruet)

352
(pepper)

(salt)

341 — $125; **342** — $210; **343** — $95; **344** — $120; **345** — $145 (S); **346** — $90; **347** — $12
348 — $100; **349** — $50; **350** — $150; **351** — $140; **352** — $38 ea.

Blown Opalescent Syrups, etc.

353
Coinspot
(9-panel)

354
Coinspot
(ring-neck)

355
Bubble Lattice·
(unfrosted)

356
Stripe·

357
Daisy & Fern
(optic mold)

358
Polka Dot

359
Swastika

360
Spanish Lace
(old reeded handle)

Opalescent Windows

361
(syrup, tall)*

362
(toothpick)

363
(sugar shaker)

364
(syrup, squatty)*

365
(salt shaker)

·It is notable that these syrups, all attributed to Hobbs, have identical lids

353 – $90; **354** – $110; **355** – $220 (S); **356** – $175 (S); **357** – $60; **358** – $175 (S); **359** – $225 (VR); **360** – $225 (R); **361** – $210; **362** – $95; **363** – $110; **364** – $175; **365** – $35.

Sugar Shakers, etc.

366
Poinsettia

367
Daisy & Fern
(Buckeye)

368
Daisy & Fern
(Northwood)

369
Daisy & Fern
(Apple Blossom mold)

370
Daisy & Fern
(alternating panels)

371
Bubble Lattice
(bulbous)

372
Bubble Lattice
(tapered)

373
Swirl
(tall)

374
Twist
(blown)

375
Leaf Mold

376
Coinspot

377
Coinspot
(ring-neck)

378
(toothpick)

379
Coinspot
(9-panel)

380
(toothpick)

381
Swirl
(short)

382
(toothpick)

366 – $135; **367** – $80; **368** – $90; **369** – $110; **370** – $125 (S); **371** – $135 (R); **372** – $130; **373** – $80; **374** – $75 (S); **375** – $185 (VR); **376** – $65; **377** – $65; **378** – $85 (S); **379** – $55*; **380** – $75; **381** – $85; **382** – $55.

Assorted Tumblers
(PRESSED & BLOWN)

383	384	385	386	387
Jewel & Flower	*Idyll*	*Panelled Holly*	*Beatty Swirl*	*Lustre Flute*

388	389	390	391
Bubble Lattice	*Seaweed*	*Daisy & Fern*	*Opal. Stripe*

392	393	394	395
Poinsettia (pressed)	*Drape* (jefferson)	*Opal. Swirl*	*Wide Stripe* (diamond quilted)

(rare green)

396	397	398	399	400
Daffodil	*Swastika*	*Spanish Lace*	*Poinsettia*	*Twist*

383 — $90 (R); **384** — $75 (S); **385** — $120 (VR); **386** — $50; **387** — $65 (S); **388** — $40 (S); **389** — $45; **390** — $32; **391** — $28; **392** — $24, **393** — $24; **394** — $28 (S); **395** — $50 (R); **396** — $45 (VR); **397** — $55 (R); **398** — $55 (R); **399** — $75; **400** — $50.

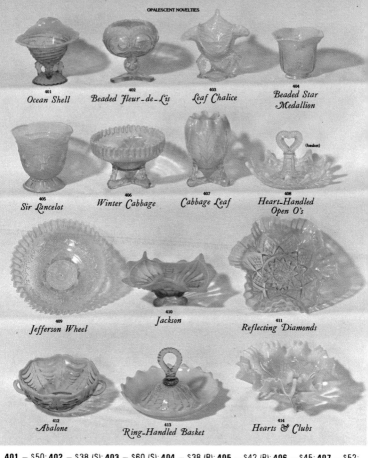

401
Ocean Shell

402
Beaded Fleur-de-Lis

403
Leaf Chalice

404
Beaded Star Medallion

405
Sir Lancelot

406
Winter Cabbage

407
Cabbage Leaf

408
Heart-Handled Open O's

(basket)

409
Jefferson Wheel

410
Jackson

411
Reflecting Diamonds

412
Abalone

413
Ring-Handled Basket

414
Hearts & Clubs

401 — $50; **402** — $38 (S); **403** — $60 (S); **404** — $38 (R); **405** — $42 (R); **406** — $45; **407** — $52;
408 — $60 (S); **409** — $35; **410** — $26; **411** — $35 (S); **412** — $28; **413** — $75 (R); **414** — $35 (S).

Dolphin Compote 415
Dolphin & Herons 416
Dolphin Petticoat 417
Dolphin Compote 415
417

Blossom & Palm 418
Daisy & Plume 419
Three Fruits 420

Three Fruits with Meander 421
Grapes & Cherries 422
Greek Key & Scales 423

Beaded Stars 424
Netted Roses 425
Bushel Basket 426

415 – $45*; **416** – $55 (R); **417** – $85; **418** – $35; **419** – $38; **420** – $60 (S); **421** – $65 (R); **422** – $48 (S); **423** – $40 (S); **424** – $30; **425** – $52 (S); **426** – $50 (S).

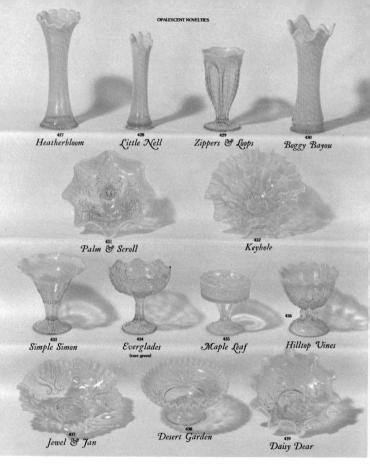

427
Heatherbloom

428
Little Nell

429
Zippers & Loops

430
Boggy Bayou

431
Palm & Scroll

432
Keyhole

433
Simple Simon

434
Everglades
(rare green)

435
Maple Leaf

436
Hilltop Vines

437
Jewel & Jan

438
Desert Garden

439
Daisy Dear

427 – $24; **428** – $26; **429** – $32; **430** – $24; **431** – $38; **432** – $35 (S); **433** – $28; **434** – $55 (S); **435** – $55 (S); **436** – $48; **437** – $30; **438** – $32 (S); **439** – $35 (S).

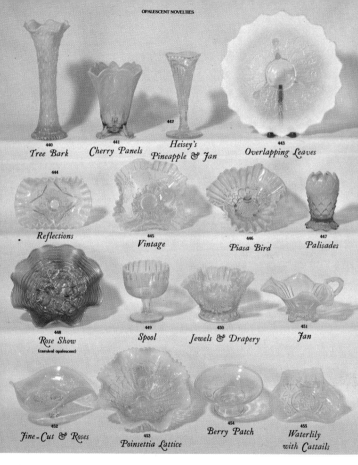

440
Tree Bark

441
Cherry Panels

442
Heisey's
Pineapple & Fan

443
Overlapping Leaves

444
Reflections

445
Vintage

446
Piasa Bird

447
Palisades

448
Rose Show
(carnival opalescent)

449
Spool

450
Jewels & Drapery

451
Fan

452
Fine-Cut & Roses

453
Poinsettia Lattice

454
Berry Patch

455
Waterlily
with Cattails

440 – $28; **441** – $60 (S); **442** – $325 (VR); **443** – $38 (Fenton); **444** – $35 (S); **445** – $35 (Fenton); **446** – $48 (R); **447** – $32; **448** – $250 (S); **449** – $28; **450** – $32; **451** – $28; **452** – $32; **453** – $65 (S); **454** – $30; **455** – $28.

456 Pearl Flowers

457 Fluted Bars & Beads

458 Maple Leaf Chalice

459 Palisades

460 Hearts & Flowers

461 Cashews

462 Spokes & Wheels

463 Blocked Thumbprint & Beads

464 Scheherezade

465 Coinspot, Pressed

466 Basketweave Base, Open-Edged

467 Beaded Cable

468 Shell & Wild Rose

469 Diamond Point & Fleur-de-Lis

470 Waterlily with Cattails

471 Lattice Medallions

456 – $22; **457** – $35; **458** – $45 (S); **459** – $22; **460** – $52 (S); **461** – $35; **462** – $32; **463** – $24; **464** – $35 (S); **465** – $24; **466** – $22; **467** – $30; **468** – $32*; **469** – $26; **470** – $55; **471** – $28.

472
Spool

473
*Aurora
Borealis*

474
*Miniature
Epergne*

475   476
Beads & Bark

477
Wishbone & Drape

478
Twister

479
Reverse Drapery

480
Fancy Fantails

481
Blackberry

482
Button Panels

483
Pearls & Scales

472 – $25; **473** – $36; **474** – $95; **475** – $48; **476** – $50 (S); **477** – $28; **478** – $32 (R); **479** – $32 (S) (Fenton); **480** – $35; **481** – $28 (Fenton); **482** – $38; **483** – $35.

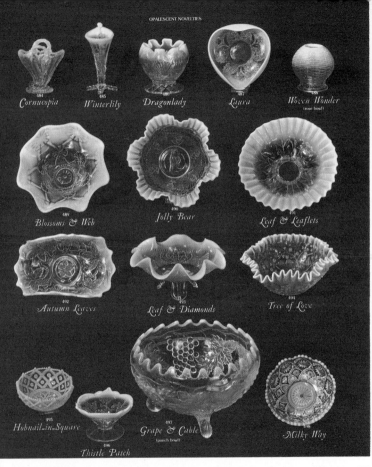

484
Cornucopia

485
Winterlily

486
Dragonlady

487
Laura

488
Woven Wonder
(rose bowl)

489
Blossoms & Web

490
Jolly Bear

491
Leaf & Leaflets

492
Autumn Leaves

493
Leaf & Diamonds

494
Tree of Love

495
Hobnail-in-Square

496
Thistle Patch

497
Grape & Cable
(punch bowl)

498
Milky Way

484 – $28 (S); **485** – $25 (S); **486** – $22; **487** – $24 (S); **488** – $25; **489** – $26; **490** – $75 (S); **491** – $22; **492** – $22; **493** – $24; **494** – $24 (R); **495** – $18; **496** – $22; **497** – $85 (R) (Fenton); **498** – $22.

499 *Corn Vase*

500 *Stork & Rushes* (mug)

501 *Opal Open* (rose bowl)

502 *Stump Mug*

503 *Grapevine Cluster*

504 *Leaf & Beads*

505 *Wheel & Block*

506 *Beads & Curly-Cues*

507 *Meander*

508 *Beaded Drapes*

509 *Jewel & Flower*

510 *Many Loops*

511 *Roulette*

512 *Ruffles & Rings*

513 *Tokyo*

499 – $85*; **500** – $45 (R); **501** – $32; **502** – $45; **503** – $50; **504** – $32; **505** – $32; **506** – $32; **507** – $28; **508** – $26; **509** – $32; **510** – $22; **511** – $28; **512** – $26; **513** – $24.

514
Northern Star
(chop plate)

515
Beaded Jan
(rose bowl)

516
Coral

517
Barbells

518
Astro

519
Carousel

520
Woven Wonder

521
Windflower

522
Popsickle Sticks

523
Sea Spray
(olive)

524
Open O's

525
*Spool &
Threads*

526
Blooms & Blossoms
(olive)

514 — $60 (S) (Fenton); **515** — $32; **516** — $36; **517** — $28; **518** — $32; **519** — $42 (S); **520** — $42 (S); **521** — $52 (R); **522** — $30; **523** — $32; **524** — $36; **525** — $28; **526** — $38.

527
Diamond
Point

528
Twisted
Ribs

529
Feathers

530
Piasa Bird

531
Fish-in-
the-Sea

532
Diamond
& Oval
Thumbprint

533
Jewels &
Drapery

534
Calyx

535
Fluted Scrolls
with Vine

536
Lined
Heart

537
Lorna

538
Diamond
Stem

539
Concave
Columns

540
Many
Ribs

541
Jefferson's
Spool

542
Beads
& Bark

543
Dahlia
Twist

544
Aurora
Borealis

545
Fluted Bars
and Beads

546
Corn Vase

527 – $28; **528** – $24; **529** – $22; **530** – $55; **531** – $45 (S); **532** – $26; **533** – $26; **534** – $48 (S); **535** – $35; **536** – $28; **537** – $22; **538** – $38; **539** – $24; **540** – $30; **541** – $26; **542** – $45; **543** – $30; **544** – $35; **545** – $36; **546** – $165 (VR)*.

English Opalescent

547
Coronation

548
Piccadilly

549

550
Crown Jewels

551
Ascot

552
Contessa

553
William & Mary

554
War of Roses

555
Chippendale

556

Richelieu

557

547 – $135; **548** – $55; **549** – $55; **550** – $135; **551** – $50; **552** – $45; **553** – $95; **554** – $38; **555** – $55; **556** – $58; **557** – $55.

Assorted Tiny Things

(toothpick holders, salt dips, etc . . .)

558
Idyll

559
Wreath & Shell
(salt dip)

560
Beatty
Honeycomb

561
Beatty Rib

562
Twist (mini. spooner)

563
Panelled Sprig

564
Shell

565
William & Mary
(master salt – English)

566
Polka Dot

567
Over - All Hob

568 **569**
Gonterman Swirl

570
Jern

571
Ring-Handle Basket

572
Reverse
Swirl
(ring neck)

573
Beaded Ovals in Sand
(nappy)

574
Tiny Twig
(vase)

(The above are not reproductions)

558 — $175 (R); **559** — $95 (R); **560** — $45; **561** — $35; **562** — $70 (S); **563** — $38; **564** — $300 (VR); **565** — $55 (S); **566** — $200 (VR); **567** — $55; **568** — $175 (S); **569** — $135; **570** — $50; **571** — $28; **572** — $35; **573** — $28; **574** — $45*.

575
Spanish Lace

576
Colonial Stairsteps

577
Jackson

578
Bullseye

579
Seaweed

580
Opal. Swirl

581

582   583
Beatty Honeycomb

584
Diamond Spearhead

585   586
Beatty Ribbed Opal

587

588
Beatty Honeycomb

589

(The above are not reproductions)

575 – $45; **576** – $95 (S); **577** – $150; **578** – $50; **579** – $45; **580** – $26; **581** – $85 (R); **582** – $30; **583** – $22; **584** – $45 (S); **585** – $22; **586** – $40 (R); **587** – $45 (VR); **588** – $30; **589** – $38.

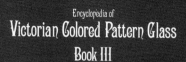

Encyclopedia of
Victorian Colored Pattern Glass
Book III

Syrups, Sugar Shakers & Cruets

From A to Z

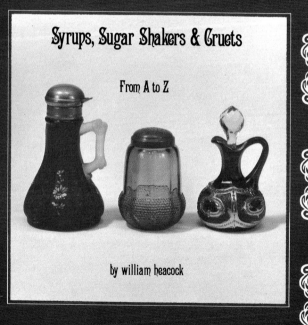

by william heacock

Photo by Jack Hall Photography

RARE EMERALD GREEN
"PINEAPPLE & FAN"
(syrup)

Value — $400

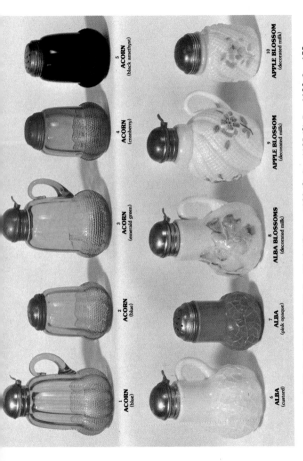

1
ACORN
(blue)

2
ACORN
(blue)

3
ACORN
(emerald green)

4
ACORN
(cranberry)

5
ACORN
(black amethyst)

6
ALBA
(custard)

7
ALBA
(pink opaque)

8
ALBA BLOSSOMS
(decorated milk)

9
APPLE BLOSSOM
(decorated milk)

10
APPLE BLOSSOM
(decorated milk)

1 – $150; 2 – $90; 3 – $135; 4 – $140 (VR); 5 – $100 (S); 6 – $195 (S); 7 – $120; 8 – $75;
9 – $145; 10 – $110.

11 ARGUS SWIRL (cranberry)

12 ARGUS SWIRL (cranberry)

13 ARGUS SWIRL (peach bloom)

14 ARGUS SWIRL (peach bloom)

15 ASTER & LEAF (blue)

16 ASTER & LEAF (emerald green)

17 AZTEC MEDALLION (SWIRL) (green opal.)

18 BANDED BARREL (amber)

19 BANDED PORTLAND (rose-flashed)

20 BASKETWEAVE (amber)

11 — $225 (S); 12 — $145; 13 — $225 (S); 14 — $125; 15 — $160 (S); 16 — $95; 17 — $175 (VR); 18 — $85 (S); 19 — $250 (S); 20 — $95.

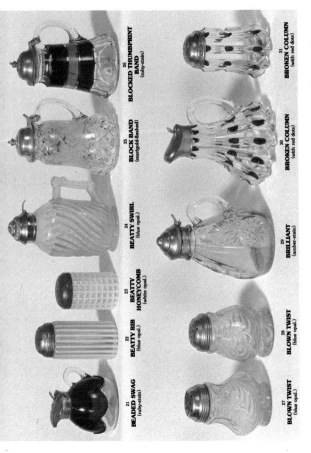

21 BEADED SWAG (ruby-stain)

22 BEATTY RIB (blue opal.)

23 BEATTY HONEYCOMB (white opal.)

24 BEATTY SWIRL (blue opal.)

25 BLOCK BAND (marigold-flashed)

26 BLOCKED THUMBPRINT BAND (ruby-stain)

27 BLOWN TWIST (blue opal.)

28 BLOWN TWIST (blue opal.)

29 BRILLIANT (amber-stain)

30 BROKEN COLUMN (with red dots)

31 BROKEN COLUMN (with red dots)

21 — $120; 22 — $65; 23 — $65 (R); 24 — $230 (R); 25 — $135; 26 — $115; 27 — $65; 28 — $75; 29 — $195 (S); 30 — $265 (R); 31 — $160 (S).

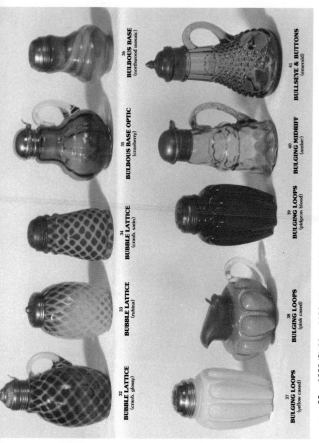

32
BUBBLE LATTICE
(cranb. glossy)

33
BUBBLE LATTICE
(rubina)

34
BUBBLE LATTICE
(cranb. satin)

35
BULBOUS BASE OPTIC
(cranberry)

36
BULBOUS BASE
(northwood mosaic)

37
BULGING LOOPS
(yellow cased)

38
BULGING LOOPS
(pink cased)

39
BULGING LOOPS
(pigeon blood)

40
BULGING MIDRIFF
(amber)

41
BULLSEYE & BUTTONS
(emerald)

32 — $300 (S); 33 — $150; 34 — $175 (S); 35 — $150; 36 — $225 (R); 38 — $210;
39 — $200 (S); 40 — $95; 41 — $175 (VR). 37 — $125 (VR)

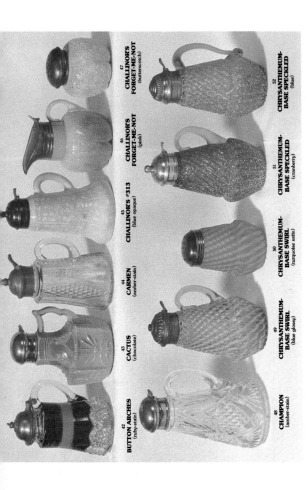

42 BUTTON ARCHES (ruby-stain)

43 CACTUS (chocolate)

44 CARMEN (amber-stain)

45 CHALLINOR'S #313 (blue opaque)

46 CHALLINOR'S FORGET-ME-NOT (pink)

47 CHALLINOR'S FORGET-ME-NOT (butterscotch)

48 CHAMPION (amber-stain)

49 CHRYSANTHEMUM-BASE SWIRL (blue glossy)

50 CHRYSANTHEMUM-BASE SWIRL (turquoise satin)

51 CHRYSANTHEMUM-BASE SPECKLED (cranberry)

52 CHRYSANTHEMUM-BASE SPECKLED (blue)

42 – $150 (S); **43** – $150; **44** – $150; **45** – $85; **46** – $120; **47** – $110 (R); **48** – $125 (S); **49** – $165; **50** – $120; **51** – $325 (R); **52** – $250 (R).

89

Coin Spot

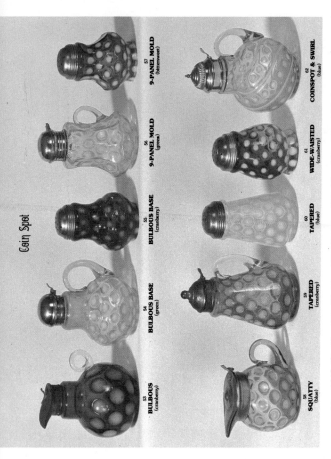

53 BULBOUS (cranberry)

54 BULBOUS BASE (green)

55 BULBOUS BASE (cranberry)

56 9-PANEL MOLD (green)

57 9-PANEL MOLD (bittersweet)

58 SQUATTY (blue)

59 TAPERED (cranberry)

60 TAPERED (blue)

61 WIDE-WAISTED (cranberry)

62 COINSPOT & SWIRL (blue)

53 — $115 (S); **54** — $95 (R); **55** — $75 (S); **57** — $75; **57** — $75; **56** — $75; **57** — $65*; **58** — $95 (R); **59** — $95;
60 — $65; **61** — $75; **62** — $90.

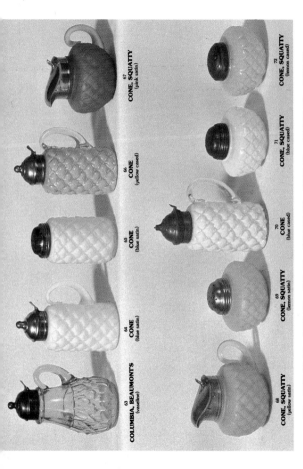

63
COLUMBIA, BEAUMONTS
(vaseline)

64
CONE
(blue satin)

65
CONE
(blue satin)

66
CONE
(yellow cased)

67
CONE, SQUATTY
(pink satin)

68
CONE, SQUATTY
(yellow satin)

69
CONE, SQUATTY
(lemon satin)

70
CONE
(blue cased)

71
CONE, SQUATTY
(blue satin)

72
CONE, SQUATTY
(lemon cased)

63 – $225 (S); **64** – $100; **65** – $75; **66** – $150 (S); **67** – $150; **68** – $160 (R); **69** – $125 (S); **70** – $125; **71** – $90; **72** – $95 (S).

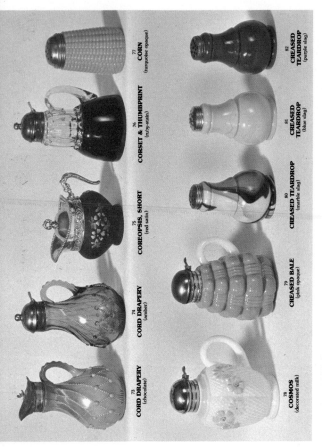

77
CORN
(turquoise opaque)

76
CORSET & THUMBPRINT
(ruby-stain)

75
COREOPSIS, SHORT
(red satin)

74
CORD DRAPERY
(amber)

73
CORD DRAPERY
(chocolate)

82
CREASED
TEARDROP
(purple slag)

81
CREASED
TEARDROP
(blue slag)

80
CREASED TEARDROP
(marble slag)

79
CREASED BALE
(pink opaque)

78
COSMOS
(decorated milk)

73 — $165 (S); 74 — $295 (R); 75 — $235 (R); 76 — $160; 77 — $75; 78 — $175; 79 — $145 (R);
80 — $65; 81 — $65; 82 — $65.

83
CRISS-CROSS
(rubina satin)

84
CURRIER & IVES
(amber)

85
DAISY & BUTTON
(sapphire blue)

86
DAISY & BUTTON
WITH CROSSBARS
(amber)

87
DAISY & BUTTON WITH
THUMBPRINT PANELS
(amber)

Daisy & Fern

88
APPLE BLOSSOM MOLD
(blue)

89
BULBOUS
(old reeded handle)

90
NORTHWOOD MOLD

91
W.VA. OPTIC MOLD
(blue)

92
WIDE-WAISTED
MOLD
(cranberry)

83 – $425 (VR); 84 – $165 (S); 85 – $175 (S); 86 – $165 (S); 87 – $150 (R); 88 – $110;
89 – $130; 90 – $140 (S); 91 – $110; 92 – $95.

93

93
DAISY IN CRISS-CROSS
(cranberry)

94
DELTA
(amber)

95
DIAMOND
SPEARHEAD
(green opal.)

96
DOUBLE THUMBPRINT BAND
(blue)

97
DRAPED GARLANDS
(ruby-stain)

98
EMPRESS
(emerald green)

99
ERIE TWIST
(glossy)

100
ERIE TWIST
(satiny)

101
FAMOUS
(apple green)

102
FEATHER
(emerald green)

93 — $350 (VR); 94 — $80; 95 — $235 (S); 96 — $95; 97 — $180 (S); 98 — $260; 99 — $200;
100 — $165; 101 — $225 (VR); 102 — $250 (VR).

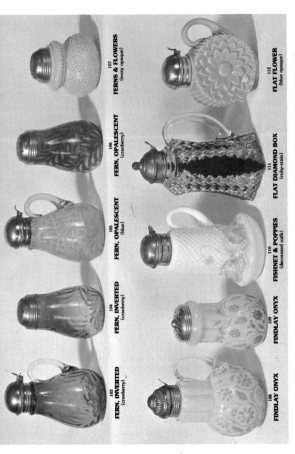

103 FERN, INVERTED (cranberry)

104 FERN, INVERTED (cranberry)

105 FERN, OPALESCENT (blue)

106 FERN, OPALESCENT (cranberry)

107 FERNS & FLOWERS (ivory opaque)

108 FINDLAY ONYX

109 FINDLAY ONYX

110 FISHNET & POPPIES (decorated milk)

111 FLAT DIAMOND BOX (ruby-stain)

112 FLAT FLOWER (blue opaque)

103 – $200; 104 – $145; 105 – $175; 106 – $175 (S); 107 – $140 (VR); 108 – $450 (VR); 109 – $250; 110 – $100; 111 – $210 (VR); 112 – $120.

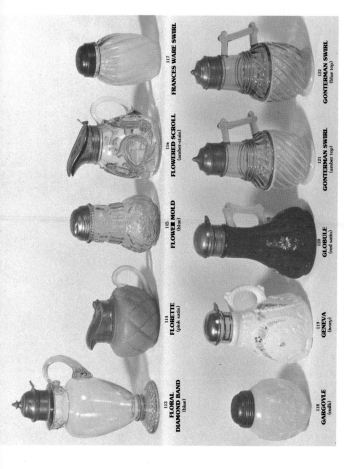

113
FLORAL
DIAMOND BAND
(blue)

114
FLORETTE
(pink satin)

115
FLOWERED MOLD
(blue)

116
FLOWERED SCROLL
(amber satin)

117
FRANCES WARE SWIRL

118
GARGOYLE
(milk)

119
GENEVA
(ivory)

120
GLOBULE
(red satin)

121
GONTERMAN SWIRL
(amber top)

122
GONTERMAN SWIRL
(blue top)

113 — $150 (S); 114 — $175 (S); 115 — $120 (S); 116 — $185 (R); 117 — $135 (S); 118 — $55 (R); 119 — $250; 120 — $450 (VR); 121 — $300 (R); 122 — $350 (VR).

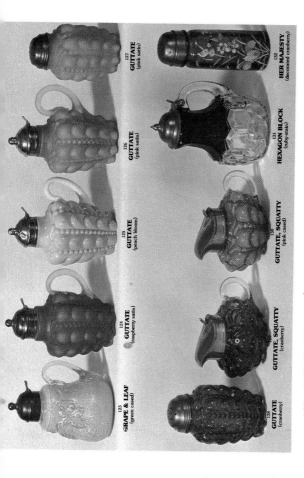

123
GRAPE & LEAF
(green cased)

124
GUTTATE
(raspberry satin)

125
GUTTATE
(peach bloom)

126
GUTTATE
(pink satin)

127
GUTTATE
(pink satin)

128
GUTTATE
(cranberry)

129
GUTTATE, SQUATTY
(cranberry)

130
GUTTATE, SQUATTY
(pink cased)

131
HEXAGON BLOCK
(ruby-stain)

132
HER MAJESTY
(decorated cranberry)

123 — $145 (S); **124** — repro; **125** — $110*; **126** — $165*; **127** — $135; **128** — $210 (S); **129** — $320 (S); **130** — $175; **131** — $135; **132** — $145 (S).

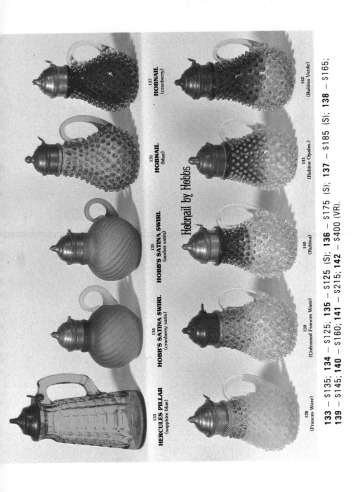

133
HERCULES PILLAR
(sapphire blue)

134
HOBB'S SATINA SWIRL
(cranberry satin)

135
HOBB'S SATINA SWIRL
(amber satin)

135
HOBNAIL
(blue)

137
HOBNAIL
(cranberry)

Hobnail by Hobbs

138
(Frances Ware)

139
(Unfrosted Frances Ware)

140
(Rubina)

141
(Rubina Opales.)

142
(Rubina Verde)

133 – $135; 134 – $125; 135 – $125 (S); 136 – $175 (S); 137 – $185 (S); 138 – $165;
139 – $145; 140 – $160; 141 – $215; 142 – $400 (VR).

143
HOBNAIL,
PRESSED
(green)

144
HOBNAIL,
PRESSED
(blue)

145
HOLLY AMBER

146
HORSESHOE
(amber)

147
HONEYCOMB, OPALES.
(blue)

148
HOURGLASS MOLD
(vaseline etched)

149
INSIDE RIBBED
(blue)

150
INVERTED THUMBPRINT
(baby)

151
IVT
(bulbous)

152
IVT
(decorated)

153
IVT
(pinched base)

143 — $60 (S); 144 — $55; 145 — $700 (R); 146 — $55; 147 — $165 (R); 148 — $85; 149 — $75;
150 — $115; 151 — $85; 152 — $175 (S); 153 — $85.

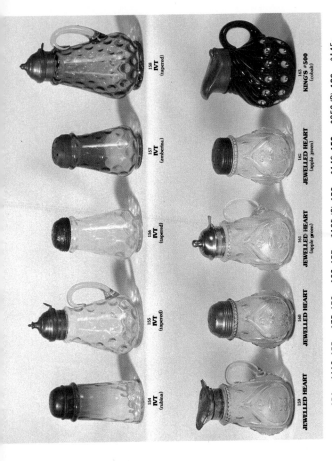

154 — $110; 155 — $75; 156 — $60; 157 — $195 (S); 158 — $140; 159 — $250 (R); 160 — $145; 161 — $220 (R); 162 — $110; 163 — $320 (VR).

158
IVT
(tapered)

163
KING'S #500
(cobalt)

157
IVT
(ambertina)

162
JEWELLED HEART
(apple green)

156
IVT
(tapered)

161
JEWELLED HEART
(apple green)

155
IVT
(tapered)

160
JEWELLED HEART

154
IVT
(rubina)

159
JEWELLED HEART

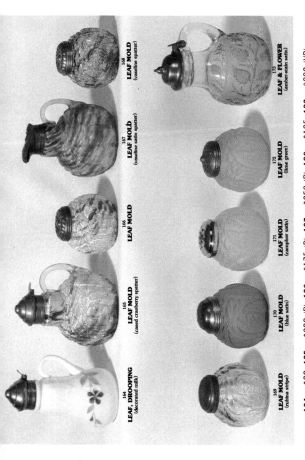

164
LEAF, DROOPING
(decorated milk)

165
LEAF MOLD
(cased cranberry spatter)

166
LEAF MOLD

167
LEAF MOLD
(vaseline satin spatter)

168
LEAF MOLD
(vaseline spatter)

169
LEAF MOLD
(rubina satin)

170
LEAF MOLD
(blue satin)

171
LEAF MOLD
(camphor satin)

172
LEAF MOLD
(lime green)

173
LEAF & FLOWER
(amber-stain satin)

164 – $60; **165** – $320 (R); **166** – $175 (R); **167** – $350 (R); **168** – $165; **169** – $220 (VR); **170** – $125 (S); **171** – $85; **172** – $150 (VR); **173** – $165 (S).

174 174
LEAF UMBRELLA
(cranberry)

175
LEAF UMBRELLA
(mauve)

176
LEAF UMBRELLA
(lemon)

177
LEAF UMBRELLA
(blue satin)

178
LEAF UMBRELLA
(cranberry spatter)

179
LEANING PILLARS

180
LEANING PILLARS

181
LEANING PILLARS

182
LITTLE SHRIMP
(ivory)

183
LITTLE SHRIMP
(turquoise blue)

184
LITTLE SHRIMP
(decorated satin)

174 – $375; 175 – $400; 176 – $125; 177 – $200 (R); 178 – $150 (S); 179 – $85 (S);
180 – $65; 181 – $65; 182 – $65; 183 – $65; 184 – $75.

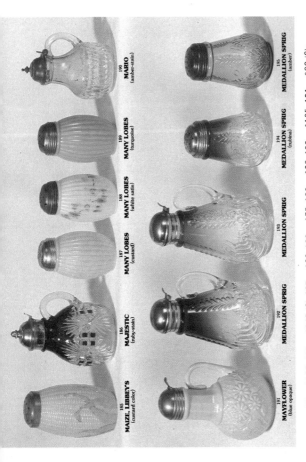

185 MAIZE, LIBBEY'S (custard color)

186 MAJESTIC (ruby-stain)

187 MANY LOBES (custard)

188 MANY LOBES (white satin)

189 MANY LOBES (turquoise)

190 MARIO (amber-stain)

191 MAYFLOWER (blue opaque)

192 MEDALLION SPRIG

193 MEDALLION SPRIG

194 MEDALLION SPRIG (nubina)

195 MEDALLION SPRIG (amber)

185 — $165; 186 — $145 (S); 187 — $60; 188 — $75; 189 — $60; 190 — $165, 191 — $90 (S); 192 — $240 (R); 193 — $240 (R); 194 — $165 (S); 195 — $175 (R).

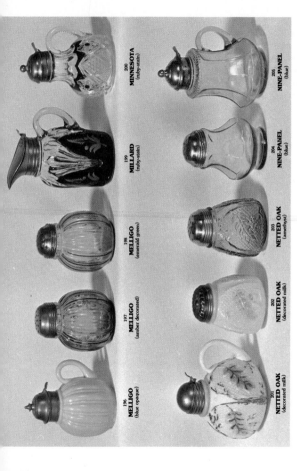

196
MELLIGO
(blue opaque)

197
MELLIGO
(amber decorated)

198
MELLIGO
(emerald green)

199
MILLARD
(ruby-stain)

200
MINNESOTA
(ruby-stain)

201
NETTED OAK
(decorated milk)

202
NETTED OAK
(decorated milk)

203
NETTED OAK
(amethyst)

204
NINE-PANEL
(blue)

205
NINE-PANEL
(blue)

196 – $75 (S); **197** – $60; **198** – $65; **199** – $145; **200** – $225 (S); **201** – $110; **202** – $85; **203** – $135 (VR); **204** – $60*; **205** – $65.

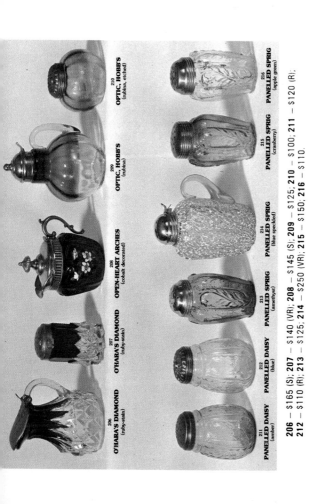

211
PANELLED DAISY
(amber)

212
PANELLED DAISY
(blue)

213
PANELLED SPRIG
(amethyst)

214
PANELLED SPRIG
(blue speckled)

215
PANELLED SPRIG
(cranberry)

216
PANELLED SPRIG
(apple green)

206
O'HARA'S DIAMOND
(ruby-stain)

207
O'HARA'S DIAMOND
(ruby-stain)

208
OPEN-HEART ARCHES
(cobalt decorated)

209
OPTIC, HOBB'S
(rubina)

210
OPTIC, HOBB'S
(rubina, etched)

206 – $165 (S); 207 – $140 (VR); 208 – $145 (S); 209 – $125; 210 – $100, 211 – $120 (R);
212 – $110 (R); 213 – $125; 214 – $250 (VR); 215 – $150; 216 – $110.

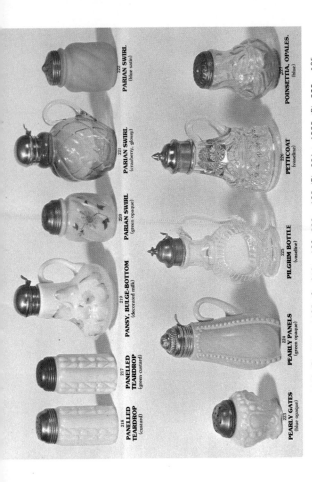

222
PARIAN SWIRL
(blue satin)

221
PARIAN SWIRL
(cranberry, glossy)

220
PARIAN SWIRL
(green opaque)

219
PANSY, BULGE-BOTTOM
(decorated milk)

217
PANELLED
TEARDROP
(green custard)

218
PANELLED
TEARDROP
(custard)

227
POINSETTIA, OPALES.
(blue)

226
PETTICOAT
(vaseline)

225
PILGRIM BOTTLE
(vaseline)

224
PEARLY PANELS
(green opaque)

223
PEARLY GATES
(blue opaque)

217 – $110 (R); 218 – $165 (S); 219 – $80; 220 – $90 (R); 221 – $225 (R); 222 – $65;
223 – $90 (VR); 224 – $90 (S); 225 – $145; 226 – $300 (S); 227 – $145 (S).

232
PORTLY PANELS
(blue)

231
POLKA DOT
(cranberry)

230
POLKA DOT
(blue)

229
POLKA DOT
(bulbous)

228
POLKA DOT
(cranberry)

237
PRISCILLA FOSTORIA'S
(emerald green)

236
PRIMA DONNA
(cranberry-spatter)
(vasa murrhina)

235
PRETTY PANELS
(amber)

234
PRESSED OCTAGON
(amber decorated)

233
PRESSED DIAMOND
(vaseline)

228 — $325 (S); **229** — $200; **230** — $160; **231** — $190; **232** — $160 (R); **234** — $85.
235 — $95 (S); **236** — $110 (R); **237** — $250 (R).

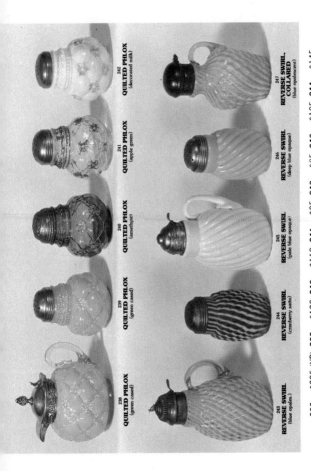

242 QUILTED PHLOX (decorated milk)

241 QUILTED PHLOX (apple green)

240 QUILTED PHLOX (amethyst†)

239 QUILTED PHLOX (green cased)

238 QUILTED PHLOX (green cased)

247 REVERSE SWIRL, COLLARED (blue opalescent)

246 REVERSE SWIRL (deep blue opaque)

245 REVERSE SWIRL (pale blue opaque†)

244 REVERSE SWIRL (cranberry satin)

243 REVERSE SWIRL (blue opales.)

238 — $225 (VR); **239** — $100; **240** — $110; **241** — $95; **242** — $85; **243** — $165; **244** — $145 (S); **245** — $95 (S); **246** — $60; **247** — $165 (R).

252
RIB, SCROLLED
(blue opaque)

257
RIDGE SWIRL
(cobalt)

251
RIBBED OPAL LATTICE
(cranberry, short)

256
RIDGE SWIRL
(amber)

250
RIBBED OPAL LATTICE
(blue)

256
RIBBED PILLAR
(blue spatter)

249
TORPEDO
(ruby-stain)

254
RIBBED PILLAR
(spatter)

248
REVERSE SWIRL
(speckled, canary)

253
RIBBED PILLAR
(spatter)

248 — $150 (S); 249 — $165; 250 — $145; 251 — $125 (R); 252 — $60; 253 — $160; 254 — $100; 255 — $145 (S); 256 — $65; 257 — $75 (VR).

258 RING BAND (custard)

259 RING NECK (spatter)

260 RING NECK (pale spatter)

261 RING NECK (spatter-IVT)

262 RING NECK (optic)

263 RING NECK (stripe, opales.)

264 RING-WAIST (decorated emerald)

265 ROBIN'S NEST (amber)

266 ROSE PETALS (pink cased)

267 ROSE PETALS (pink satin)

258 – $250 (S); **259** – $100; **260** – $60; **261** – $65, **262** – $65; **263** – $250 (S); **264** – $95; **265** – $160 (S); **266** – $285 (R); **267** – $325 (IVR).

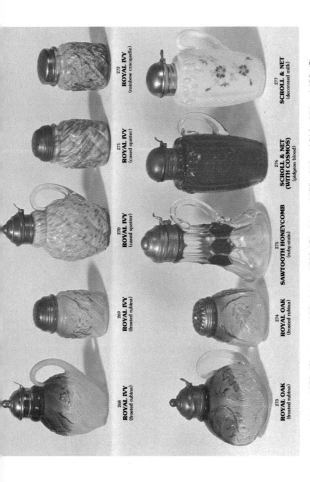

268
ROYAL IVY
(frosted rubina)

269
ROYAL IVY
(frosted rubina)

270
ROYAL IVY
(cased spatter)

271
ROYAL IVY
(cased spatter)

272
ROYAL IVY
(rainbow craquelle)

273
ROYAL OAK
(frosted rubina)

274
ROYAL OAK
(frosted rubina)

275
SAWTOOTH HONEYCOMB
(ruby-stain)

276
SCROLL & NET
(WITH COSMOS)
(pidgeon blood)

277
SCROLL & NET
(decorated milk)

268 – $375 (S); **269** – $135; **270** – $500 (R); **271** – $175; **272** – $210; **273** – $450 (R); **274** – $165; **275** – $225 (R); **276** – $375 (VR); **277** – $75.

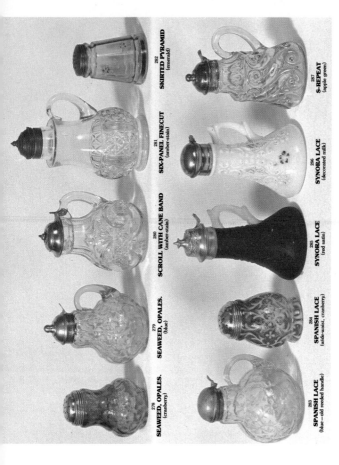

278
SEAWEED, OPALES.
(cranberry)

279
SEAWEED, OPALES.
(blue)

280
SCROLL WITH CANE BAND
(amber-stain)

281
SIX-PANEL FINECUT
(amber-stain)

282
SKIRTED PYRAMID
(emerald)

283
SPANISH LACE
(blue—old reeded handle)

284
SPANISH LACE
(wide-waist, cranberry)

285
SYNORA LACE
(red satin)

286
SYNORA LACE
(decorated milk)

287
S-REPEAT
(apple green)

278 — $165 (S); 279 — $225; 280 — $175 (S); 281 — $165 (R); 282 — $60; 283 — $220 (R); 284 — $135; 285 — $425 (VR); 286 — $80; 287 — $225 (S).

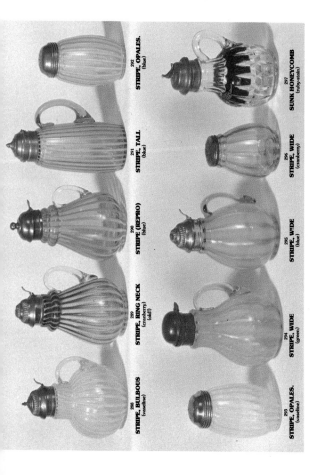

292
STRIPE, OPALES.
(blue)

291
STRIPE, TALL
(blue)

290
STRIPE (REPRO)
(blue)

299
STRIPE, RING NECK
(cranberry)
(odd!)

288
STRIPE, BULBOUS
(vaseline)

297
SUNK HONEYCOMB
(ruby-stain)

296
STRIPE, WIDE
(cranberry)

295
STRIPE, WIDE
(blue)

294
STRIPE, WIDE
(green)

293
STRIPE, OPALES.
(vaseline)

288 – $135 (R); **289** – $265 (S)*; **290** – New; **291** – $140; **292** – $110 (S); **293** – $110 (R); **294** – $160 (R); **295** – $150 (VR); **296** – $130; **297** – $140.

113

298
SUNSET
(blue opaque)

299
SWASTIKA
(green opalescent)

300
SWIRL, CAMPHOR

301
SWIRL, OPALES.
(cranberry)

302
SWIRL, OPALES.
(cranberry)

303
SWIRL, OPALES.
(bulbous base)

304
SWIRL, OPALES.
(bulbous base)

305
SWIRL, OPALES.
(Northwood)

306
SWIRL, OPALES.
(tapered)

307
SWIRL & LEAF
(white opaque)

298 — $120; 299 — $300 (VR); 300 — $75; 301 — $135; 302 — $90; 303 — $95 (R); 304 — $95 (R); 305 — $100 (VR); 306 — $90; 307 — $65 (R).

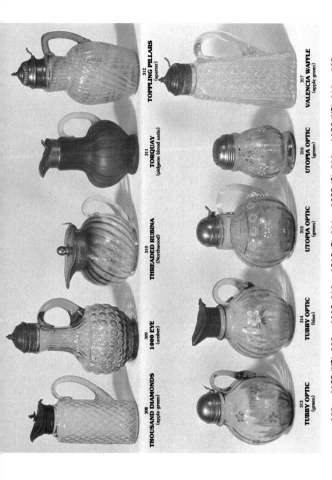

312
TOPPLING PILLARS
(spatter)

317
VALENCIA WAFFLE
(apple green)

311
TORQUAY
(pidgeon blood satin)

316
UTOPIA OPTIC
(green)

310
THREADED RUBINA
(Northwood)

315
UTOPIA OPTIC
(green)

309
1000 EYE
(amber)

314
TUBBY OPTIC
(blue)

308
THOUSAND DIAMONDS
(apple green)

313
TUBBY OPTIC
(green)

308 — $135 (VR); **309** — $110; **310** — $210 (R); **311** — $325 (S); **312** — $150 (VR); **313** — $85; **314** — $95; **315** — $90; **316** — $65; **317** — $100.

318 VENECIA (cranberry)

319 VENECIA (green to clear)

320 VENETIAN DIAMOND (cranberry)

321 VENETIAN DIAMOND (ring neck)

322 VENETIAN DIAMOND (spatter)

323 VICTORIA, RIVERSIDE (ruby-stained)

324 VINING ROSE (murranese)

325 WEDDING BELLS (rose-flashed)

326 WEST VIRGINIA OPTIC (amethyst)

327 WEST VIRGINIA OPTIC (green)

318 – $85; 319 – $75; 320 – $135; 321 – $110; 322 – $115; 323 – $250 (S); 324 – $165
(S); 325 – $135; 326 – $90 (S); 327 – $65 (S).

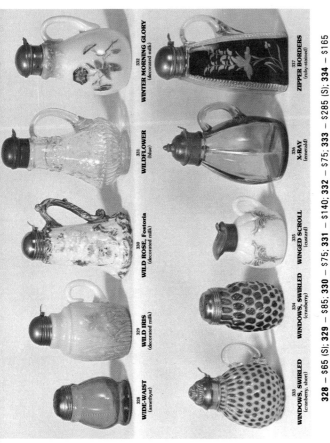

328
WIDE-WAIST
(amethyst)

329
WILD IRIS
(decorated milk)

330
WILD ROSE, Fostoria
(decorated milk)

331
WILDFLOWER
(blue)

332
WINTER MORNING GLORY
(decorated milk)

333
WINDOWS, SWIRLED
(cranberry, short)

334
WINDOWS, SWIRLED
(cranberry)

335
WINGED SCROLL
(custard)

336
X-RAY
(emerald)

337
ZIPPER BORDERS
(ruby-stained)

328 — $65 (S); 329 — $65 (S); 330 — $85, 330 — $75; 331 — $140; 332 — $75; 333 — $285 (S); 334 — $165 (S); 335 — $225; 336 — $265 (VR); 337 — $135 (S).

117

New England Glass Examples

338 BULBOUS SATINA

339 COCKLESHELL

340 EGG, MT. WASHINGTON

341 EGG—BASED (Belleware)

342 EGG—BASED (Belleware)

347 OSTRICH EGG

346 TOMATO

345 SMITH BROTHER'S MELON

344 GILLINDER MELON

343 FIG

338 — $160; 339 — $500 (VR); 340 — $175; 341 — $135; 342 — $145; 343 — $350 (S); 344 — $125; 345 — $200 (S); 346 — $175; 347 — $315 (R).

Late Additions

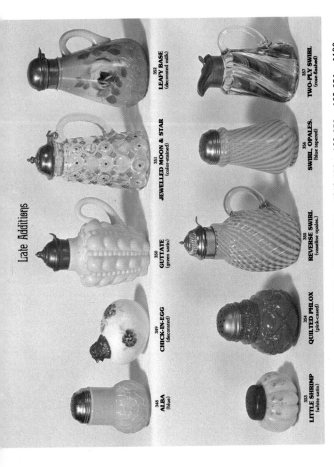

348 ALBA (white satin)

349 CHICK-IN-EGG (decorated)

350 GUTTATE (green satin)

351 JEWELED MOON & STAR (color-stained)

352 LEAFY BASE (decorated milk)

353 LITTLE SHRIMP (blue)

354 QUILTED PHLOX (pink-cased)

355 REVERSE SWIRL (vaseline opales.)

356 SWIRL, OPALES. (blue tapered)

357 TWO-PLY SWIRL (rose-flashed)

348 — $90; 349 — $550 (VR); 350 — $135 (VR); 351 — $210; 352 — $60; 353 — $90; 354 — $120; 355 — $165; 356 — $110; 357 — $150.

Milk Glass Syrups
(& sugar shaker)

358 PANELLED SPRIG (H)	**359** ENCIRCLED SCROLL (H)	**360** ELONGATED DROPS (W)	**361** FOSTORIA'S #1008 (H)	**362** PEARLY PANELS & FLOWER (Fostoria #1009) (H)	**363** BANDED SHELLS (H)

364 RIBS OVER RIBS (H)	**365** DITHRIDGE #25 (H)	**366** NETTED RIBBONS (H)	**367** DOUBLE RIB (M)	**368** WEST VIRGINIA'S OPTIC (K)

369 KNOTTY BULB (P)	**370** PRIMROSE & PEARLS (H)	**371** KNOBBY (M)	**372** RINGS & RIBS (H)	**373** FANCY FANS (H)

Names by: (H) Author, (W) Warman, (M) Millard, (K) Kamm, (P) Peterson

*No test provided on the above.

358-373 All items shown above — $50-$65 each.

Milk Glass Syrups

374
ROSE-IN-RELIEF
(H)
Fostoria

375
LACY FLORAL
(K)
tall

376
FRENCH PRIMROSE
(H)

377
CHAIN & SWAG
(H)

378
GIANT DOGWOOD
(H)

379
SERENDIPITY
(H)

380
STRAWBERRY PATCH
(H)

381
**FRENCH FLEUR-
DE-LIS**
(H)

382
BEADED HEXAGON
(H)

383
HIDING BUTTERFLY
(H)

384
STIPPLED DAHLIA
(P)

385
LACY FLORAL
(K)

386
PETUNIA SWIRL
(H)

387
CATHERINE ANN
(H)

Names by: (H) Author, (W) Warman, (M) Millard, (K) Kamm, (P) Peterson

*No text provided on the above.

374-387 All items shown above $50-$65 each.

Late Additions

388
ACORN DIAMONDS
(amber)
U.S. Glass – 1891

389
FLOWER MOLD
(green)

390
INVERTED THUMB-
PRINT
(decorated)

391
LIBBEY'S MAIZE
(decorated opal)

392
QUILTED PHLOX
(pink opaque)

393
RIBBED OPAL LATTICE
(tall)

394
RIDGE SWIRL
(green)

395
ROPE & RIBS
(amber)

396
ROPE &
THUMBPRINT
(blue)

397
ROPE &
THUMBPRINT
(amber)

398
SUNSET
(custard)

399
WILDFLOWER
(amber)

400
(satin scenic
decorated)

401
(spatter)

402
(tortoise shell)

403
(vaseline decor.)

404
(blue spatter)

405
(cranberry decorated)

The Hobb's Coloratura Series

388 – $95 (R); **389** – $85 (S); **390** – $110; **391** – $275 (R); **392** – $150 (R); **393** – $120; **394** – $60; **395** – $70 (S); **396** – $90; **397** – $90; **398** – $200 (R); **399** – $155; **400** – $145 (R); **401** – $125; **402** – $145; **403** – $145; **404** – $130; **405** – $165.

Fig. #405-A
Decorated opaque "COREOPSIS", tall

Fig. #405-B
Unfrosted pigeon blood "TORQUAY"

Fig. #405-C
Extremely rare amber-stained "ROYAL IVY"

Fig. #405-D
Rare Blue Opalescent "POINSETTA"

405A – $165; **405B** – $325 (R); **405C** – $275 (VR); **405D** – $325 (VR).

FIG. #405-E
OPALESCENT DIAMONDS
(Hobbs—1880's)

FIG. #405-F
FOSTORIA'S PRISCILLA

FIG. #405-G
COINSPOT & SWIRL
(Northwood Mold)

405E – $175 (S); 405F – $210 (VR); 405G – $285 (R).

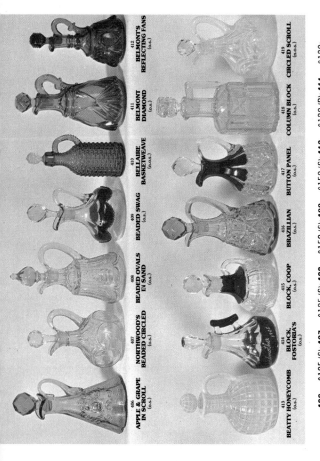

406
APPLE & GRAPE
IN SCROLL
(o.s.)

407
NORTHWOOD'S
BEADED CIRCLED
(o.s.)

408
BEADED OVALS
IN SAND
(o.s.)

409
BEADED SWAG
(o.s.)

410
BELLAIRE
BASKETWEAVE
(n.o.s.)

411
BELMONT
DIAMOND
(o.s.)

412
BELMONT'S
REFLECTING FANS
(o.s.)

413
BEATTY HONEYCOMB
(o.s.)

414
BLOCK,
FOSTORIA'S
(o.s.)

415
BLOCK, COOP
(o.s.)

416
BRAZILIAN
(o.s.)

417
BUTTON PANEL
(o.s.)

418
COLUMN BLOCK
(o.s.)

419
CIRCLED SCROLL
(n.o.s.)

406 − $185 (S); **407** − $185 (S); **408** − $135 (S); **409** − $150 (S); **410** − $120 (R); **411** − $120;
412 − $100; **413** − $195 (R); **414** − $75; **415** − $95; **416** − $135; **417** − $165; **418** − $150;
419 − $145 (VR).

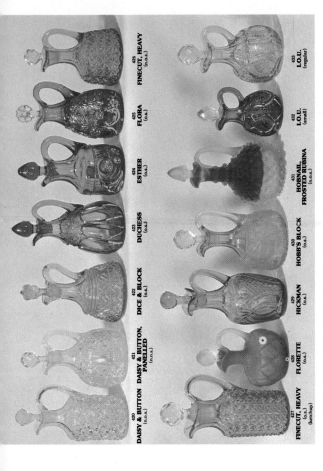

420 DAISY & BUTTON (n.o.s.)

421 DAISY & BUTTON, PANELLED (n.o.s.)

422 DICE & BLOCK (o.s.)

423 DUCHESS (o.s.)

424 ESTHER (o.s.)

425 FLORA (o.s.)

426 FINECUT, HEAVY (n.o.s.)

427 FINECUT, HEAVY (o.s.) (ketchup)

428 FLORETTE (o.s.)

429 HICKMAN (o.s.)

430 HOBB'S BLOCK (o.s.)

431 HOBNAIL, FROSTED RUBINA (n.o.s.)

432 I.O.U. (small)

433 I.O.U. (regular)

420 − $130; 421 − $140 (R); 422 − $125; 423 − $210 (S); 424 − $225; 425 − $160; 426 − $100; 427 − $100; 428 − $200 (S); 429 − $150; 430 − $200 (S); 431 − $325 (R); 432 − $90; 433 − $110.

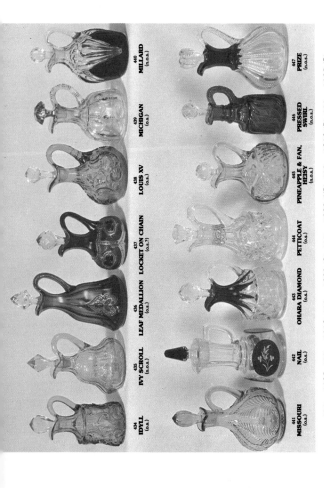

434
IDYLL
(o.s.)

435
IVY SCROLL
(n.o.s.)

436
LEAF MEDALLION
(o.s.)

437
LOCKET ON CHAIN
(o.s.?)

438
LOUIS XV
(o.s.)

439
MICHIGAN
(o.s.)

440
MILLARD
(n.o.s.)

441
MISSOURI
(o.s.)

442
NAIL
(o.s.)

443
OHARA DIAMOND
(o.s.)

444
PETTICOAT
(o.s.)

445
PINEAPPLE & FAN,
HEISY
(n.o.s.)

446
PRESSED
SWIRL
(n.o.s.)

447
PRIZE
(n.o.s.)

434 — $125; 435 — $110; 436 — $300 (S); 437 — $800 (VR); 438 — $210 (R); 439 — $185 (R);
440 — $140; 441 — $165 (R); 442 — $195 (R); 443 — $185; 444 — $200; 445 — $220 (S);
446 — $95; 447 — $185.

PATTERN INDEX

A

Abalone, 70
Acorn, 6, 85
Acorn Burrs & Bark, 20
Acorn Diamonds, 122
Alabama, 6
Alaska, 44
Alba, 85, 119
Alba Blossoms, 85
Amberette, (see Klondyke)
Apple Blossom, 85
Apple & Grape In Scroll, 125
Arabian Nights, 60
Arched Ovals, 6
Argonaut Shell, 6, 51, 52
Argus Swirl, 86
Art Novo, 6
Ascot, 80
Aster & Leaf, 86
Astral (See Beaded Star & Medallion)
Astro, 78
Atlanta, 6
Aurora Borealis, 75, 79
Autumn Leaves, 76
Aztec Medallion (Swirl), 86

B

Baby Coinspot, 63
Banded Barrel, 86
Banded Portland, 7, 86
Banded Shells, 120
Barbells, 78
Basketweave, 86
Basketweave Base, 74
Bead & Scroll, 7
Bead Swag. 7
Beaded Grape, 7
Beaded Swag, 7, 87
Beaded Oval in Sand, 7, 81, 125
Beaded Cable, 74
Beaded Circle, Northwood, 125
Beaded Drapes, 77
Beaded Fan, 78
Beaded Fleur-de-Lis, 70
Beaded Hexagon, 121
Beaded Panel & Sunburst, 7
Beaded Star & Medallion, 70
Beaded Stars, 71
Beaded Swirl & Disc, 7
Beads & Bark, 75, 79
Beads & Curley-Cues, 77

Beatty Honeycomb, 8, 55, 82, 87, 125
Beatty Rib, 8, 51, 56, 82, 87
Beatty Swirl, 46, 47, 54, 87
Bellaire Basketweave, 7, 125, 129
Belmont Diamond, 125
Belmont's Reflecting Fans, 125
Berry Patch, 73
Bevelled Star, 8
Big Daisy (See Poinsetta, Opalescent)
Blackberry, Northwood, 75
Block, Fostoria, 125
Block Band, 87
Block, Coop's 125
Blocked Midriff (See Regal, Northwood)
Blocked Thumbprint & Beads, 74
Blocked Thumbprint Band, 8, 87
Blooms & Blossoms, 78
Blossoms & Palms, 75
Blossoms & Web, 76
Blown Twist; 3-16, 51, 59, 60, 87
Blue Opal (See Fern, opalescent)
Bohemian, 8
Boggy Bayou, 72
Box-In-Box, 8
Brazillian, 8, 125
Brilliant, 9, 87
Britannic, 9
Broken Column, 87
Bubble Lattice, 24, 53, 54, 57, 58, 59, 60, 88
Bulbous Base, 9, 88
Bulbous Based Coinspot, 90
Bulbous Ring Neck, 9
Bulbous Satina, 118
Bulging Loops, 9, 88
Bulging Midriff, 88
Bullseye Opalescent, 53, 94
Bullseye & Buttons, 88
Bushel Basket, 71
Button Arches, 9, 89
Button Panel, 9, 125
Button Panels, 75
Button Panel With Bars, 9
Buttons & Braids, 52, 36

C

Cabbage Leaf, 70
Cactus, 10, 89
Calyx Vase, 79
Candy Stripe (Stripe, Opales.)
Carmen, 89
Carnation, 39
Carnations & Pleats (See Ruffles & Rings)
Carousel, 78
Cashews, 74
Catherine Ann, 121
Chain & Swag, 121
Challinor's #313, 89
Challinor's Forget-Me-Not, 17, 89, 129
Champion, 10, 89
Cherry Panels, 73
Chick-in-Egg, 119
Chippendale, 80
Christmas Bowl (See Poinsettia Lattice)
Christmas Pearls, 54
Christmas Snowflake, 64
Chrysanthemum Base Speckled, 10, 89
Chrysanthemum Base Swirl, 24, 59, 89
Chrysanthemum Leaf, 10
Chrysanthemum Spring, 10, 129
Circled Scroll, 47, 82, 125
Cockleshell, 118
Coin, 10
Coinspot, 60, 67, 68, 90
Coinspot & Swirl, 63, 90, 124
Coinspot, Pressed, 74
Colonial Stairsteps, 82
Colorado, 10
Coloratura, 122
Columbia, Beaumont's, 11, 91
Columbian Coin, 11
Column Block, 125
Concave Columns, 79
Cone, 11, 91
Consolidated Criss-Cross, 24, 60, 64, 3-22
Contessa, 80
Coral, 86
Cord Drapery, 11, 92
Cordova; 11

Coreopsis, 92, 123
Corn Vase, 77, 79
Corn, 92
Cornell, 12
Cornucopia, 76
Coronation, 92
Corset & Thumbprint, 92
Cosmos, 92
Creased Bale, 12, 92
Creased Teardrop, 92
Croesus, 12, 40, 129
Crown Jewels, 80
Currier & Ives, 93
Curtain Call, 54
Cut Block, 12

D

Daffodils, 69
Dahlia Twist, 79
Daisy & Button, 13, 93,
  126, 3-22, 55
Daisy & Button, Panelled,
  126
Daisy & Button With Cross-
  Bar, 93
Daisy & Button With
  Thumbprint, 93
Daisy & Cube, (See Stars
  & Bars)
Daisy & Fern, 24, 60, 62,
  63, 66, 67, 68, 69, 93
Daisy & Plume, 71
Daisy Dear, 72
Daisy in Criss-Cross, 64, 94
Delaware, 12
Delta, 94
Desert Garden, 72
Diamond & Oval
  Thumbprint, 79
Diamond Point Vase, 79
Diamond Points & Fleur-
  de-Lis, 74
Diamond Peg (See
  Diamond with Peg)
Diamond Spearhead, 12
  51, 54, 55, 56, 82, 94
Diamond Stem, 79
Diamond with Peg, 14
Diamonds, Opales., 124
Dice & Block, 126
Dithridge #25, 120
Dogwood (See Art Novo)
Dolly Madison, 52
Dolphin & Herons, 71
Dolphin Compote, 71
Dolphin Petticoat, 71
Double Arch, 14

Double Circle, 14, 129
Double Dahlia With Lens, 14
Double Greek Key, 52, 56, 40
Double Rib, 126
Double Thumbprint Band, 94
Doyle's Honeycomb, 14
Dragonlady, 76
Draped Beads, 14
Draped Garland, 94
Drapery, Northwood, 50
Duchess, 55, 126
Duncan & Miller #42, 40

E

Egg, Mt. Washington, 118
Ellipses, 14
Elongated Drops, 120
Empress, 3-23, 15
Encircled Scroll, 120
English Hob Band (See
  Lustre Flute)
Erie Twist, 94
Esther, 15, 126
Eureka, National's, 15
Everglades, 45, 57, 49
Expanded Diamond (See
  Ribbed Opal Lattice)
Expanded Stem, (See Calyx
  Vase)

F

Famous, 15, 94
Fan, 73, 51
Fancy Fans, 120
Fancy Fantails, 75
Fancy Loop, 15
Fans With Crossbars,
  (See Champion)
Feather, 15, 94
Feathers, 79
Fern, Inverted, 95
Fern Opales., 24, 62, 63,
  66, 95
Fern Ribbed, 24
Ferns & Flowers, 95
Fig, 118
Findlay Onyx, 62, 95
Finecut, Heavy, 126
Finecut & Roses, 36, 73
Finecut Medallion (See
  Austrian)
Fish-In-The-Sea (Vase), 79
Fishnet & Poppies, 95
Flat Diamond Box, 95
Flat Flower, 95
Flat Panel (See Pleating)
Fleur-de-Lis (See Iris With
  Meander)

Flora, 15, 56, 57, 126
Floradora (See Bohemian)
Floral Diamond Band, 96
Florette, 16, 96, 120
Flower & Bud (See Blooms
  & Blossoms)
Flower & Pleat, 16
Flower Mold, 96, 122
Flower Spray & Scrolls
  (See Intaglio)
Flowered Scroll, 96
Flute, 16, 52
Fluted Bars & Beads, 74, 79
Fluted Scrolls, 50, 57
Fluted Scrolls With Flower
  Band (See Jackson)
Fluted Scrolls With Vine, 79
Forget-Me-Not, Challinor's,
  17, 3-18
Fostoria #1008, 120
Frances Ware Hobnail, 19, 98
Frances Ware Swirl, 17, 96
Frazier, 17
French Primrose, 121
Frosted Leaf &
  Basketweave, 49

G

Galloway, 36
Gargoyle, 96
Geneva, 17, 96
Georgia Gem, 17
Giant Dogwood, 121
Gillinders Melon, 118
Globule, 96
Gold Band, 18
Gonterman Hob., 53
Gonterman Swirl, 3-25, 18,
  54, 55, 81, 96
Grape & Cable, 76
Grape & Cherry, 71
Grape & Leaf, 97
Grapevine Cluster, 77
Greek Key & Scales, 71
Guttate, 18, 97, 119

H

Harvard, 18
Heart, 19
Heart-Handled Open-O's, 70
Hearts & Clubs, 70
Hearts & Flowers, 74
Heatherbloom, 72
Her Majesty, 97
Hercules Pillar, 98
Herringbone, Opales., 62, 64
Hexagon Block, 97

131

Hickman, 39, 126
Hiding Butterfly, 121
Hilltop Vines, 80
Hobb's Block, 126
Hobb's Satina Swirl, 98
Hobnail, 19, 65, 53, 98, 126, 98
Hobnail & Panelled Thumbprint 49, 58
Hobnail, 4-Footed, 53
Hobnail, Hobbs, 19, 65, 53, 98, 126
Hobnail-In-Square, 53
Hobnail, Northwood, 53
Hobnail, Pressed, 99
Hobnail (Reproductions), 2-91
Hobnail, 3 Footed (See Over—All Hob)
Holly Amber, 19, 99
Honeycomb & Clover, 34
Honeycomb, Opalescent, 61, 3-28
Honeycomb With Flower Rim (See Vermont)
Horseshoe, 99
Hourglass Mold, 99

I

I.O.U., 126
Idyll, 19, 52, 55, 69, 81, 127
Inside Ribbed, 99
Inside Ribbing, 27
Intaglio, 46, 51, 57
Interlocking Crescents (See Double Arch)
Inverted Fan & Feather, 20, 46
Inverted Thumbprint, 20, 99-100
Iowa, 1-46
Iris (See Wild Bouquet)
Iris With Meander, 20, 52, 57
Ivy, Sandwich, 21
Ivy Scroll, 127

J

Jackson, 50, 56, 70, 82
Jefferson #212 (Tokyo), 36, 2-24
Jefferson #231 (Double Circle), 14, 129
Jefferson #249 (Finecut & Roses), 2-66
Jefferson #250 (Ribbed Drape)
Jefferson #251 (See Idyll)

Jefferson #264 (Carousel), 78
Jefferson Coinspot, 2-43
Jefferson Spool, 79
Jefferson Wheel, 70
Jewel & Fan, 72
Jewel & Flower, 45, 52, 57, 77
Jewelled Heart, 21, 52, 55, 57, 100, 129
Jewelled Moon & Star, 119
Jewels & Drapery, 73, 79
Jolly Bear, 76
Jubilee (See Hickman)

K

Kentucky, 21
King's Crown (See Ruby Thumbprint)
King's #500, 100
Kittens, 1-28
Klondike, 21
Klondyke (See Fluted Scrolls)
Knobby, 120
Knotty Bulb, 120

L

Labelle Opal, 1-32
Labelle Rose (See Rose Show)
Lacy Floral, 121
Lacy Medallion, 21
Lattice & Daisy (See Christmas Snowflake)
Lattice Medallions, 74
Laura, 76
Leaf & Beads, 77
Leaf & Diamond, 76
Leaf & Flower, 101
Leaf & Leaflets, 76
Leaf & Star, 21
Leaf Bracket, 21
Leaf Chalice, 70
Leaf Drooping, 101
Leaf Medallion, 127
Leaf Mold, 22, 68, 101
Leaf Umbrella, 22, 102
Leafy Base, 119
Leaning Pillars, 102
Lined Heart, 79
Lion, Late (See Atlanta)
Little Gem (See Georgia Gem)
Little Nell, 72
Little Shrimp, 102, 119
Locket on Chain, 127
Log & Star, 129

Lorna, 79
Louis XV, 127
Lustre Flute, 58, 69

M

Maize, Libbey's, 23, 103, 122
Majestic, 23, 103
Many Lobes, 103
Many Loops, 77
Many Ribs, 79
Maple Leaf (Northwood), 23, 56, 72
Maple Leaf Chalice, 74
Mario, 103
Mayflower, 103
Meander, 77
Medallion Sprig, 23, 103
Melligo, 104
Melon (Smith Bros.), 3-47
Milky Way, 76
Michigan, 127
Millard, 104, 127
Miniature Epergne, 75
Minnesota, 39, 104
Missouri, 127
Moon & Star, 2-91

N

Nail, 127
Nautilus (See Argonaut Shell)
Nestor, 23, 129
Netted Roses, 71
Netted Oak, 104
Netted Ribbons, 120
New Hampshire, 23
Nine-Panel, 104
Northern Star, 78
Northwood Coinspot, 2-43
Northwood's Block, 37

O

Ocean Shell, 70
O'Hara Diamond, 105, 127
Old Man Winter (Basket), 38
One-O-One, 23
Onyx, Findlay, 2-45, 3-24
Opal Open, 77
Open-Heart Arches, 105
Open O's, 78, 70
Optic, Hobb's, 27, 105
Optic, Pressed (See Inside Ribbing)
Optic, West Virginia's, 3-45, 27
Orange Tree (Repro.), 2-91
Orinda, 27
Ostrich Egg, 118

Over-All Hob, 27, 53, 81
Overlapping Leaves, 73

P

Palisades, 73, 74
Palm & Scroll, 72
Palm Beach, 51
Palm Leaf, 28
Panelled Daisy, 105
Panelled Holly, 47, 49
Panelled Sprig, 34, 81, 105, 120
Panelled Teardrop, 106
Panelled Zipper (See Iowa)
Pansy, 28
Pansy, Bulge Bottom, 106
Parian Swirl, 28, 106
Peacocks On A Fence, 38
Pearl Flowers, 74
Pearls & Scales, 75
Pearly Gates, 106
Pearly Panels, 106
Pearly Panels & Flower, 120
Petalled Medallion (See Brilliant)
Petticoat, 28, 106, 127
Petunia Swirl, 121
Piasa Bird, 73, 79
Piccadilly, 80
Picket, 28
Pilgrim Bottle, 106
Pillar, Ribbed (See Ribbed Pillar)
Pine Apple, 29
Pineapple & Fan (Heisey), 29, 73, 84, 127
Plaid (See Bubble Lattice)
Plain Scalloped Panel, 29
Pleating, 29
Poinsetta, Opales., 3-35, 60, 61, 68, 69, 106, 123
Poinsetta Lattice, 73
Polka Dot, 25, 67, 81, 107
Popsickle Sticks, 78
Portly Panels, 107
Pressed Diamond, 107
Pressed Optic (See Inside Ribbing)
Pressed Octagon, 107
Pressed Swirl, 127
Pretty Panels, 107
Prima Donna, 29
Primrose & Pearls, 120
Prince Albert, 29
Prince of Wales Plumes, 29
Priscilla (Fostoria), 107, 124
Prize, The, 30, 127

Pump & Trough (novelty), 38
Punty Band, 30

Q

Queen's Lace (See Spanish Lace)
Quilt (See Florette)
Quilted Phlox, 30, 108 119, 122

R

Reflecting Diamonds, 70
Reflections, 73
Regal (Northwood), 51, 52
Reverse Drapery, 75
Reverse Swirl (Opalescent or Speckled), 3-37, 26, 30, 57, 59, 61, 63, 64, 81, 108, 109, 119
Rib, Eight (See Bulging Loops)
Rib & Bead, 30
Rib Scrolled, 109
Ribbed Basket (See Ribbed Spiral)
Ribbed Coinspot, 2-43
Ribbed Drape, 30
Ribbed Opal Lattice, 25, 59, 66, 109, 122
Ribbed Pillar, 29, 109
Ribbed Spiral, 30, 48, 54, 56
Ribbed Swirl (See Gonterman Swirl)
Ribs over Ribs, 120
Richelieu, 80
Ridge Swirl, 109, 122
Ring Band, 31, 110
Ring Base, 31
Ring-Handled Basket, 81
Ring Neck (Mold) 9, 25, 27, 110
Rings & Ribs, 120
Ring-Waist Base, 110
Robin's Nest, 110
Rope & Ribs, 122
Rope & Thumbprint, 122
Rose Petals, 110
Rose, Pink, 3-39
Rose-In-Relief, 121
Rose Show, 73
Roulette, 77
Royal, Coop's, 31
Royal, King's, 31
Royal Ivy, 31, 111, 123

Royal Oak, 32, 111
Ruby Thumbprint, 32
Ruffles & Rings, 77

S

S-Repeat 34, 47, 51, 129, 112
Sawtoothed Honeycomb, 111
Saxon, 32, 128
Scalloped Daisy (See Diamond With Peg)
Scalloped Six-Point, 32
Scalloped Skirt, 32, 129
Scalloped Swirl, 32
Scheherezade, 74
Scroll & Net, 111
Scroll With Acanthus, 33, 47, 55, 57
Scroll With Cane Band, 33, 112
Sea Spray, 78
Seaweed, 25, 57, 59, 62, 69, 82, 112
Serendipity, 121
Serrated Ribs & Panels, 33
Shamrock Souvenir (Toothpick), 33
Shell, 33, 52, 55, 56, 81, 128
Shell & Dots (See Beaded Fan)
Shell & Seawood, 41
Shell & Wild Rose, 74
Shell & Wreath (See Wreath & Shell)
Shoeshone, 33, 128
Simple Simon (Vase), 72
Sir Lancelot, 78
Six-Panel Fine-Cut, 3-41
Skirted Pyramid, 3-41
Spanish Coin (See Columbian Coin)
Spanish Lace, 25, 61, 63, 64, 66, 67, 69, 82, 112
Spearpoint Band, 34, 128
Sprig, Panelled (See Panelled Sprig)
Spokes & Wheels, 74
Spool, 73, 75
Spool Of Threads, 78
Stars & Bars, 39, 129
Stippled Dahlia, 121
Stork & Rushes (Mug), 77
Strawberry Patch, 121
Stripe, Opales., 25, 60, 62, 67, 69, 113
Stripe, Wide, 26, 69, 113

Summit, The 34
Sunbeam, 34
Sunburst-On-Shield, 54; 55
Sunk Honeycomb, 34, 113
Sunset, 51, 34, 113, 122
Sunken Primrose (See
    Florida)
Swag With Brackets, 35, 49,
    51
Swastika, Opales., 3-43, 63,
    67, 69, 114
Swirl, Camphor, 114
Swirl, Opales., 26, 62-64,
    68-69, 82, 119.
Swirl, Princess, 35
Swirl, Two-Ply, 35, 119
Swirl & Leaf, 35, 114
Swirling Maze, 61
Synora Lace, 112

T

Tacoma, 39, 128
Texas, 41
Thistle Patch, 76
Thompson's #77, 35, 128
Thousand Diamonds, 115
Thousand Eye, 35, 53, 115,
    128
Threaded Rubina Swirl,
    41, 115
Three Fruits, 79
Three Fruits With Meander,
    71
Thumbprint, Tarentum's, 35
Tiny Optic, 35, 129
Tokyo, 36, 51, 52, 57, 77
Tomato, 118
Tooth & Claw (See Esther)

Torpedo, 109
Torquay, 115, 123
Toppling Pillars, 115
Town Pump (See Pump &
    Trough)
Tree of Life (See Challinor
    #313)
Tree of Love, 76
Tree Stump Mug, 78
Tree Trunk (Vase), 73
Truncated Cube, 35, 128
Tubby Optic, 115
Twig, Tiny, 81
Twist, 36, 81
Twist, Blown, 60, 68, 87
Twisted Ribs (Vase), 79
Twister, 75

U

U.S. Rib, 36, 128
Utopia, Optic, 115

V

Valencia Waffle, 115
Venecia, 116
Venetian Diamond, 36, 116
Vermont, 36
Vesta, 2-21, 92
Victoria Riverside, 116
Vining Rose, 116
Vintage, 73
Virginia, 1-58, 7

W

War of Roses, 80
Washington, 36
Waterlily With Cattails, 52,
    55, 75
Wedding Bells, 37, 116

West Virginia's Optic, 27,
    116, 120
Wheel & Block, 77
Wheel & Gate (See
    Jefferson's Wheel)
Wide Stripe (See Stripe,
    Wide)
Wide Waist (Mold), 117
Wild Bouquet, 37, 45, 55,
    57
Wild Iris, 117
Wild Rose, Fostoria's, 117
Wild Rose With Scrolling, 37
Wildflower, 117, 122
William & Mary, 80
Windflower, 78
Windows, Opales., 26, 62,
    67, 64, 117
Winged Scroll, 3-46, 37
Winter Cabbage, 70
Winterlily, 76
Winter Morning Glory, 117
Wishbone & Drapery, 75
Woven Wonder, 76, 78
Wreath & Shell, 38, 48

X

X-Ray, 38, 117, 128

Y

York Herringbone (See
    Scalloped Swirl)

Z

Zanesville, 38
Zenith, 128
Zipper Borders, 117
Zipper Slash, 38
Zippers & Loops, 72